JUST ONE MORE DAY

Deborah Pearson

Just One More Day

Deborah Pearson

FIRST ENERGY THERAPEUCTIC SOLUTIONS EDITION, 2017, San Clemente, CA 92673

Visit our website at www.etsforyou.com

ISBN: 0996662227

ISBN 9780996662222

Library of Congress Control Number: 2016920450

DEDICATION

I dedicate this book to my beloved husband, Chuck Pearson and my wonderful children and their families.

ACKNOWLEDGEMENTS

This book is dedicated to the memory of my beloved husband, Chuck Pearson. I am also deeply appreciative and I have the deepest love for my four children and their spouses, whom have helped me through the hardest time of my life while also enduring their own grief. Through their love and support, I had the strength to go on in my life. They mean everything to me and I am so thankful for their gift of love and their love of family.

I am also deeply grateful for my dear friend and business partner, Barbara Mahaffey, M.A. She has supported me through my toughest times with her love, understanding and kindness. Barbara has taught me, over the years, how to use the energy that surrounds and fills all of us and helps us stay clear and centered, especially during our most difficult challenges.

Many thanks go out to my wonderful brother, my brother and sister in laws and my dear friends whom have loved and supported me during my time of grief. I am so grateful to them and I have been very blessed with all the love and support from family and friends.

CONTENTS

Acknowledgements   v
Introduction   ix

Chapter 1   That Fateful Day
             July 30, 2007   1
Chapter 2   Coping with the Diagnosis   10
Chapter 3   Surgery   18
Chapter 4   What's Next   36
Chapter 5   Dealing with Cancer   49
Chapter 6   Remission "A Monumental Day"   70
Chapter 7   The Last few Days   90
Chapter 8   What Now?   96

Section II   105
Chapter 9   Grieving   107
Chapter 10   Moving Forward   118
Chapter 11   My Final Thoughts   132

INTRODUCTION

After the incredibly devastating loss of my husband in 2008, I decided to write a book about my experience. The purpose of this book is to help others understand that grief is hard and our experiences are all unique and yet alike in so many ways.

I am telling you my story because I want to share how I experienced my caregiving and my grief in hopes that you will find some comfort during your own times of grief.

Sharing how I managed to get through the worst experience of my life and what helped me regain the will to live will hopefully help you understand how grief can affect us. Also, how what I learned gave me hope, confidence and endurance to help sustain the pain and exhaustion I was going through.

I learned that I could shift out of my overwhelming grief even though I didn't think I could, or even want to, into a better frame of mind where I could function and endure. Even though I felt so powerless to deal with my grief, the use of energy work and meditating and my love for Chuck, helped me so much. It also helped my husband, my children and myself. It gave me the strength to do what I had to.

My experience made me aware of how deeply grief affects people and what a difficult transition grief can be. I experienced emotions that I never knew existed. My life and awareness of things around me changed dramatically.

Sharing my ups and downs of my husband's lung cancer diagnosis, treatments, challenges and results were very difficult for me because not only do I want to help others overcome their grief, but also I needed to overcome mine. Writing about my experience was a healing process for me.

After two years of writing about my experience, I felt an incredible release of emotions when I finished my book.

In this book, I am going to take you through my journey from the beginning to the end and all the challenges I faced along the way. Most importantly,

I will share with you the lessons and techniques I learned to help me deal with my experience and my emotions.

Over 35 years ago, I learned all about how our thoughts affect our lives and how to use energy to help us heal, cope and change detrimental habit patterns and beliefs that I had. This was essential is learning how to perceive and handle everything that I was going through.

I learned about energy and how it deeply affects us, our health, our thoughts and how it keeps our minds and our bodies in harmonious balance. Aligning with high frequency energies causes positive thoughts and helps our body to heal. Chuck and I both used these techniques so much every day.

One of the most important concepts that we used daily was aligning with low (negative) energy frequencies which causes negative thoughts, which greatly impedes our body and our mind's natural ability to heal.

Another concept that was so important is understanding how energy affected everything in life. I studied how our bodies and mind are designed and structured to use energy and how to improve every aspect of my life, mentally, emotionally, biochemically and situationally. Everything that exists is made of different energy frequencies (our minds, plants, the sun, our thoughts, our bodies, the sky, the earth, everything).

I learned how to meditate and use these high frequency energies both for my mind and my body, which helped my family and myself through all kinds of challenges.

I learned how the appropriate use of different kinds of energy creates health, balance, and harmony in our minds and in our body. I knew everything that exists is energy but I didn't know that you could use energy to help yourself. I also didn't know that we are designed and structured to be able to use energy so effectively.

I was not aware that the body had so many different types of energy systems such as; energy pathways called meridians, also that each organ and body part has its own energy frequencies and that they all interact with each other.

We, as human beings, are innately structured to utilize all types of energy in our daily functioning. We are born with the ability to work with our body's natural energy systems and it is natural, once learned, how to align with powerful energies that help us manifest what we want, internally and externally.

What is Energy?

Everything that exists is made of energy. Like the sun, trees, plants, your thoughts, water, your body and the air, etc. Everything has its own unique vibratory level or frequency to function optimally.

As I mentioned, I had no idea you could use energy to change your state of mind or heal your body. I soon found out that energy is easy to work with and align with to give you the results that you want.

For example: When I learned how to raise my vibratory level I started thinking positive thoughts and my mind and body began to heal.

And...

When I started thinking negative thoughts, as I often did during this time, it detrimentally affected my mental, emotional, physical health and well-being.

Dark thoughts equal low frequencies. Low frequency causes your body and mind not to work properly. Positive thoughts equal high frequencies, which helps the body to naturally heal itself.

How I used Energy to help myself through this tough time.

Once I understood what energy was, I learned how to use it to help my husband and myself, especially when the physical and emotional pain was difficult to handle, which was often.

When I was thinking negative thoughts, I learned how to expand my energy to create positive thoughts and feelings instead. Then I became aware that my body and mind automatically started healing. I noticed how much it helped my husband when he could see and feel the difference in me. He also learned how to use energy to help him feel better and to deal with the whole situation along with the intense physical pain that the cancer caused.

Using the energy techniques daily made a huge difference in both of our lives and it gave us a feeling of understanding about our own innate powers and how we can use them to make our lives better.

Who knew you could do that!

CHAPTER 1
THAT FATEFUL DAY
JULY 30, 2007

I t all began as an ordinary day. We woke up, showered and had breakfast and Chuck kissed me goodbye. His words to me every morning were, "I love you and HAVE A NICE DAY". That was his signature statement.

Life seemed to be rolling along with the normal highs and lows except one day out of the clear blue Chuck started having some severe lower back and hip pain. This wasn't unusual for him because years ago he slipped a disk and since then his back pain has been an ongoing challenge. Considering his experience with his back, he was not overly concerned and went about his normal work schedule.

A few months later, the pain was still there. He had been going to the chiropractor, his doctor, and having acupuncture treatments. The chiropractor appointments did help a little, but the chronic ache remained. This was typical for him and not too different than the other times when his back hurt and he needed a chiropractic adjustment. The difference this time was that the pain was getting worse instead of improving even after all these treatments.

It was now three months later and still no relief. He could not go on any longer so he called his doctor again but this time he wanted to explore more thoroughly what could be wrong.

It appeared that everyone, including doctors and chiropractors, thought it was his sciatic nerve, a common back problem. The pain began in April, 2007 and was chronic for those three months but nothing was helping and he realized that this could be more serious than just back pain.

Chuck made an appointment with his doctor to explore the situation more closely. When he arrived at the doctor's office, the doctor ordered X-rays and then Chuck left and went back to work. By the time he returned to his office, which was about 25 minutes away, he received a call from his doctor asking him to return to the office immediately. Chuck's response to the doctor was that he had too much work to do and didn't have time to return to the doctor's office but his doctor insisted. In Chuck's mind, he thought why is this doctor making me come all the way back to the office. He could not comprehend that anything serious was wrong but of course, he drove back to see his doctor immediately. The results of the X-rays were shocking.

Sadly, enough, this turned out to be one of the worst days of our lives. I was extremely oblivious to what was happening because I thought, as Chuck did, that the back pain was nothing serious and so I didn't give it a second thought. At this point, I had no idea what was happening.

Then out of the blue, while I was driving home from an appointment, I get this strange phone call from Chuck. He asked me to please meet him at our house because we needed to talk about something. I thought to myself, how strange is this, but never in my wildest dreams, did I imagine for one minute that what I was going to hear would change our lives forever.

When I arrived at home, Chuck was sitting on the couch looking forlorn and in shock. I sat down next to him still not aware that he was going to share anything as serious as what he told me.

It began with the story about the doctor visit and how he had to return to his doctor's office, which I thought odd but still it didn't click. Chuck said, "After going to the doctor today his doctor asked him to return immediately to his office."

His doctor looked sad and was very concerned when Chuck arrived. The reason his doctor looked so sad was because two years ago when Chuck met the doctor for the first time, ironically he told him, "Please do whatever it takes to keep me healthy and alive for a long time because I have a lot to accomplish and I want to enjoy my grandchildren. I want to travel and live a long, healthy life." I thought that was an unusual comment or could it have been an intuitive response he wasn't even aware of?

Considering Chuck's previous request to his doctor, it was even harder for his doctor to share the results of his X-Rays.

It all began with these horrible words, "CHUCK, YOU HAVE CANCER. I am sad to tell you that the cancer has already metastasized to your bones." These words were not only a shock but they were terrifying. We thought to ourselves that this just couldn't be true and this is not happening. One day he is fine with a little back pain and the next day he has late stage cancer. Not us, not Chuck, he was too healthy, outgoing, passionate and he was bigger than life.

When the diagnosis was explained to Chuck, he was told that there was a tumor on his right femur bone. The doctor explained to Chuck the extreme seriousness of this diagnosis. Chuck was then told that until the tumor was removed and sent to pathology there was no way to tell where the cancer had originated. The doctor let Chuck know that his bones were weak and he would need to use crutches from this point on. Chuck was in total shock and disbelief. Even though he was in shock, his reaction was very strong, determined and confident that he would beat it and he would have a miraculous outcome.

When I got home, Chuck was sitting on the couch and he looked so sad and confused. I walked over to the couch to sit next to him. Then he told me the shocking news. As I listened to his words, I could not imagine this to be true. I felt as though someone had hit me with a bat and knocked me out. My mind was not wrapped around his diagnosis and I couldn't believe that this was happening to us. Chuck was strong and healthy and hardly ever sick a day in his life. This was a man who wanted to live to the old age of at least 95 and he had so much more to do. I didn't believe it! Words can't explain the shock I felt. This couldn't be true and if it was, we would BEAT IT. Cancer would not win and we would fight this together as a family.

Our family was strong and determined to fight Chuck's cancer. They believed he would beat it. They also realized that we had a choice in how we could perceive and handle this situation. They were very positive and supportive. We knew we could choose being overwhelmed, sad and powerless or strong, confident and positive. In our minds, there was no other choice for us! Although we forged forward with every ounce of strength, hope, courage and love that we had, there were still so many moments that we both fell back into our fears. We also experienced many moments of overwhelming doubt.

Chuck was one of those men who carried himself with such presence and confidence that you always knew when he was in the room. His voice was so powerful and strong that you could hear him across the room and everyone knew he was there. He was the kind of man who had such determination to succeed in business. He gave wholeheartedly with every fiber of his being, all the love he had to his family. He worked day and night to support his family so we could have a nice lifestyle. Over the years he started many successful businesses. He loved to laugh and he loved to work and he especially liked to think outside the box. He had so much integrity, honor and love, which was obvious by the life he lived.

We were so stunned and shocked by the cancer diagnosis, that we couldn't eat, laugh, work, talk, or basically do anything normal. I was feeling overwhelmed with fear, denial, plus the feeling of a total loss of control.

Then after feeling all these negative emotions for a few weeks, suddenly there was a wave of intensity that reminded me of the decision I made to be strong instead of weak. My mind started thinking of all the ways I could help him. From traditional medical to holistic ways and now I had to focus only on my husband's healing. I begin the process of reading, researching, and contacting every health professional I thought might help us.

Another wave of emotion I was experiencing was the realization that nothing in the world mattered anymore except the love I had for Chuck and my family. External goods and things had no meaning. Life became more precious and I felt more of an understanding of the world and life or to better explain it, I had such an intense awareness of everything around me. I felt so much more alert and aware of how much love we had. I guess I always thought I was appreciative of family and life, but not like I was feeling now. It was different and so clear.

Everything else was a means to an end and in so many ways, this was an awakening of every part of my being. From the mind's ability to deny the reality of the diagnosis, to the spiritual strength God gave us as a family.

CHAPTER 2
COPING WITH THE DIAGNOSIS

I just couldn't begin to imagine what our lives were going to be like from this point on, not knowing what would happen, what to do and how to cope. Who Am I? How could I control the outcome because I needed him here with me for a very long time? I knew that from this moment on, life was never going to be the same. We had both been living a very full, happy, healthy and fun-filled life.

We had lots and lots of laughter and love in our daily lives. We were blessed with four wonderful children who were now between the ages of 26 and 31 and we were very busy and always on the go. Suddenly, there was this drastic change and our lives were now halted like a train coming to a complete stop while going 1,000 miles an hour. I felt like someone punched me in the stomach and I couldn't breathe.

The shock was so intense from the moment of the diagnosis, that we couldn't talk, sleep, eat or even think. We still had no idea what the next step would be and we also didn't know the severity of the disease.

Did we believe the doctor when he said that this was extremely serious? Did we believe him when he said that Chuck would not only need an operation to remove most of the tumor as soon as possible, but that his cancer wasn't curable, only treatable?

NO! NO! NO! We didn't believe the seriousness… not at all. It was too much to handle. We both believed in the power of positive thinking and that we are totally in charge of our lives. We were also both very strong and stubborn and we would never give up. We both knew and practiced the art of meditating and doing energy work. Having practiced these energy techniques for over 35 years, we felt strongly that thinking positively and never giving up would do the trick. We also felt that doing energy work including meditation, eating healthy and thinking good thoughts would give us the best chance of healing. We also counted on his doctors to find the right treatments to keep Chuck alive. We needed their expertise and we needed each other and our family more than ever. Chuck and I were lucky and blessed to have an incredible family who believed as we did.

One of the first things we did to begin the healing process, was to choose the movies and books from our own library that might help us cope and think positive thoughts. Two of those movies were, The Secret and What the Bleep Do You Know? These movies helped in keeping our attitudes positive. These movies helped in keeping our attitudes positive and explained why we think negative versus positive thoughts so watching them would help us keep our focus on healing. We started re-reading all our self-help books, meditating, and working with energy. Believe me, that made a tremendous difference in how we handled the next part of this experience. We both had a strong faith and church was part of our lives too. Between God, family, each other and keeping our attitudes positive along with the intense will to live, how could we lose?

As I mentioned, during the first two weeks we didn't sleep a wink and it was very strange being awake all day and all evening and not feeling tired but just feeling numb!

By the end of the month, we realized that we had 3-4 hours of sleep for two weeks and no sleep for the next two weeks. We walked around speechless and in shock and we were like zombies living in this dream that couldn't be real.

Since sleeping was almost non-existent and even talking to each other or anyone else was difficult, we don't know how we managed to survive this far. We laid in bed just holding hands and looking at each other not sure what to say or how to talk about it.

We felt as though we had lost all sense of reality and we also felt as though we were losing our minds.

As I mentioned earlier in the book, from the moment that Chuck and I found out about his cancer, nothing else in the world mattered to us except our love and our children. We had owned many businesses which, at times, brought lots of stress and success into our lives over the years but in hindsight that was nothing in comparison to this new kind of stress. We found that until this moment, we were finally able to let the business stresses disappear. The only thing left now was to focus on healing and not think about cancer being a stress but an opportunity to learn and grow and become even closer to each other.

It was so important now for us to stay focused on the positive, the good thoughts and keep our mind centered and on the goal of healing. We did this by using our energies to meditate and heal.

Nothing was worth worrying about or being concerned about because the only thing that mattered was for us to beat this cancer. The diagnosis immediately changed our lives and we became two different people. Now we only saw the best in each other and we were committed to beating this disease together as a family. Our relationship was good and we had a great love and soul connection, but we were still a normal couple with strong personalities and we knew how to fight and get angry. We worried about business and our children and our life wasn't perfect, but we were blessed in the life we had up to now and we had no regrets because we truly enjoyed our life. We had so much to be thankful for.

I must say I was a hopeless romantic as a young girl and always dreamed of the perfect love, a fairy tale love. I always wanted a truly unconditional love, but life wasn't perfect and we weren't perfect either. We came to this marriage with our own personal issues and sometimes that caused us pain. Thirty-four years of marriage and being together for 38 years taught us so much. We were best friends and always shared similar dreams and hopes. We loved hard and we fought hard. Being two first born children and two Capricorns, we could be strong headed at times but we always came back together fighting for that perfect union of two soul mates.

Chuck had a very strong faith in God and Jesus and he talked about his connection with Jesus through this whole ordeal. His faith grew stronger during this time and I admired him for that. My faith became more of a begging for God to save him. I lost sight of everything except saving his life. My focus at times was so strong that I even left my children out at times not realizing how that could be hurtful to them.

We strongly believed in the power of the mind and the energies of the universe. We didn't always practice what we preached, but we understood that we were responsible for our lives and that we create the life we want through our thoughts and actions. We found when using the universal energy, we could create positive results in our lives when we truly believed we could. When we both aligned with the energies to reduce his physical pain, we found that his pain was greatly reduced. We were quite surprised at how effective using these techniques were in lessening his pain from intense to being bearable.

The higher we kept our energy frequencies and the more positive the thoughts were, the clearer our thinking and behavior was. This allowed us to function normally once again.

I believe we all have the power to know and change things for the better but learning how to access this power can be hard until you understand how to. Many years ago, I had the feeling deep inside something bad was going to happen in my life during my 50's. I shared this intuitive experience with Chuck and he didn't take it seriously.   It always haunted me, but I didn't want to believe it could be true.   So, I pushed it to the back of my mind and used the excuse I was wrong but I didn't understand why I kept feeling this way. I had no idea at the time that it would one day come true.

CHAPTER 3
SURGERY

M oving into the next phase for Chuck meant it was time to have the tumor on his right femur bone operated on and removed. His doctor helped Chuck find a surgeon in our area to do this operation. He was told there were only two doctors in our area that had the expertise to operate and remove the tumor and one of the surgeons was at Stanford Hospital in Palo Alto, California. His surgeon told me that during the operation he would be able to determine where the cancer originated so they could move to the treatment stage.

The surgeon at Stanford agreed to see him within the next two weeks. Nothing had changed in our reality because we were still in shock and walking around like zombies. Facing this reality was still so far-fetched we just went through the motions but had no grip on what was happening.

The next two weeks felt like an eternity. It felt like a long time to wait for the operation considering the late stage of his cancer. The plan was to remove the tumor, or as much of the tumor as possible and to find out where the cancer originated which would tell us what type of cancer he had and then the oncologist could proceed with the appropriate treatments.

Also, at the appointment with the surgeon, we were told the cancer had spread (metastasized) to the femur bone in his right leg and that was the reason for all the pain. The tumor was 10 centimeters and that explained why walking became so difficult. If was very important at this point for Chuck not to break any bones, therefore, he would need to use crutches all the time. He would also need to wear a brace until the surgery.

This was one of those moments that I was completely aware of how his surgeon was feeling because I could see it in the surgeon's eyes that he didn't have much hope for Chuck as he spoke to us.

Chuck and I were very much in love and the fear and pain showed in our faces in such a way that all the nurses, doctors and even office staff would look at us with such compassion and concern that it gave me chills. They tried to be so unemotional and not affected by us (which I assume is their way of coping with terminal patients) but they couldn't help it. We were told by one of the nurses that they never saw two "old" people more in love. (We were only 55 years old so obviously, very young nurse). I could feel it in my heart that they didn't want to openly show us their emotions and it was obvious that this was hard on them too. I can't imagine getting to know your patients and connect with them knowing the outcome doesn't look good. I feel for these doctors and nurses and it helps me understand how they try to keep their distance and emotions out of the process.

We had scheduled Chuck's surgery in two weeks. Chuck's bones were fragile and weak, so wearing the brace was a necessity. It was very important that he did not break any bones before the surgery, as it could be fatal. This made us a little more terrified. What was happening to us?

It was now just a few days before the surgery and Chuck lost his balance because his bones were weakening and he fell down our stairs. He was alone at the time and when I returned home shortly thereafter, he explained that after falling down the steps, he saw stars and a bright light. He said he knew at that moment he was going to live longer and this was not his time. After telling the doctor about his fall, we realized he could have died. The surgeon told us that he was very lucky with the first fall, but if he were to fall again, it would most likely be fatal. Now it was only four days until surgery and he could not fall again so we were very careful and extremely worried. Walking was even harder and the pain getting to be unbearable.

I was so frightened and scared. We were both still in shock and I was experiencing emotions never felt before in my life. Life around me changed. I could not feel anything but fear, overwhelm and pain. Nothing in the world mattered anymore... where I lived, what possessions I owned, what was happening around me. I couldn't laugh, read, smile or barely talk to anyone either. I found myself looking at my husband with such deep and intense love. I was void of all the outside emotions that cause couples to find fault with each other, or be annoyed or upset. None of that existed anymore and I only felt pure, unconditional love for this man. I needed and wanted him with me for a long time and could not imagine life without him.

SURGERY DAY

We woke up early since we needed to be at the hospital at 5 a.m. We had not slept more than 2-3 hours a night this last month so you can imagine our exhaustion. Lately, exhaustion and shock were part of our everyday life. We began our days with prayers and energy work to help us cope with what was happening. I have never felt such fear, fear of the unknown, fear of possibly losing Chuck and fear of hearing more bad news. To think that each day was now the longest and toughest days of our lives was becoming too common. Poor Chuck laid in bed every night moaning in pain and even the medicine didn't alleviate this pain.

Our minds began playing all sorts of tricks on us and we kept thinking what if this bad thing happens or that bad thing happens. The fear made me feel so numb that I thought I was going to collapse. Thank God, I was aware that someone was watching over us and giving us the strength to wake up, face the day and keep myself and Chuck thinking as many positive thoughts as possible. I could feel God touching us by sending us light and love to keep us continuing on...

Our lives were changing rapidly and I became Chuck's primary caregiver which meant I was his nurse, wife, chauffeur, assistant, cook, researcher and anything else he needed me to be. Even though I was happy to do this, it was exhausting and I was sad. Where did all the tears come from and how many tears does a person have? Well, through those tears, I felt a strong sense of urgency and complete motivation that our love and determination would bring us through this horrific time in our lives. That is not to say that I wasn't scared and extremely worried about how someone like me, who had no knowledge in the world of cancer, could possibly put together a team of healers that could help me get Chuck through this experience and continue to remain strong as I tried to find a way to cure him.

Morning arrived and it was time to drive us to the hospital. I helped him into a wheelchair since he could not walk on his own for the last few weeks. I remember heading down the hall to the operating room feeling so frightened. Our nerves were shot and the fear showed on our faces.

I held his hand and stayed with him until they gave him the necessary medications for surgery. I was then asked to leave the room so I went into the waiting room. This was the beginning of a long road ahead. The day felt like it would never end as I stared out the window and just cried and prayed all day. The first hour went by and I remember thanking God because that was a good sign according to what the surgeon told me that the longer the surgery, the better chance of removing most of the tumor. The next hour went by and I began pacing the hospital floors and continuing to stare out the window. I was not one to cry easily in my life but I think that today I was making up for all the years without tears.

Well, the next few hours went by and finally the surgeon appeared. It was almost four and a half hours later. The surgeon told me that he had removed most of the tumor but they had trouble finding the origin of the cancer so we needed to wait until pathology sent the results back to the surgeon which should take a few more days.

I was still in the waiting room for another two hours before they could find him a room. Finally, he was taken to a room by 4 p.m. that day. Chuck was groggy and in quite a bit of pain. I sat with him for another five hours and then decided to go home and get some sleep so I could wake up early and get back to the hospital. The operation was considered a success but what did that mean at this point?

Driving home from the hospital was a blur and walking into the house without Chuck was so traumatizing, I could barely get through the door. I could not sleep because I was exhausted and frightened. I managed to collapse in the bed from total exhaustion and before long it was 7 a.m. I woke up showered and dressed and I continued to put make up on and do my hair every day during this long ordeal so I felt some feelings of normalcy and hoped that this would keep Chuck's spirits up.

When I went home each night I found my heart pounding and the tears flowing. How could I cope – what do I do to help myself keep my attitude positive and keep from falling apart. I believe in meditating and connecting with my angels and God. Thank

God I found a new peace in that connection. I also needed to think positive and since I enjoyed watching the movie, The Secret many times before his diagnosis, that now became my movie of choice every evening when I arrived home before falling asleep. This movie gave me the strength to keep positive and fill my mind with good thoughts before bed.

Morning arrived and I was off to the hospital. The nurse told me that Chuck had an episode the night before and since I don't like hospitals and being naïve as I was about them, panic set in. The nurses were wonderful and helped me calm down before I went into his room. They thought he had a heart problem but it turned out it was just a digestive issue. He did lose quite a bit of blood and needed a transfusion. That frightened me because I had never experienced this before. It turns out that this can be common when having any type of orthopedic surgery. That calmed me down a bit but this was not the best way to start my day.

When he woke, he was in severe pain even though he was heavily medicated. After about four days in the hospital and being there from early morning to late in the evening, a nurse told me I should go to the cafeteria to have some food and to go outside for some fresh air. When I came back from being outside and I opened the door to Chuck's room, before me stood one of the doctors and the look on his face made me cringe. I wanted to scream. I looked at Chuck's face and knew at that moment the news was going to be terrible.

Yes, the news was the worst imaginable. Chuck was diagnosed with fourth stage, non-small cell lung cancer. He had smoked for a few years between the ages of 18 and 24 but never after that. The oncologist said that those few years of smoking did not contribute to the fact that he had lung cancer and that there were many patients with lung cancer who did not smoke. The oncologist explained to us that the cancer was treatable, not curable and it would depend on how his body responded after the treatments on how long he would live.

After many days in the hospital we were both sure it was time to go home but that didn't happen. Chuck's leg was so swollen after the operation that he needed more care and physical therapy. I wanted to take him home and take care of him but the doctor told us that he needed to go to a rehab center until he could do more on his own.

I had less than 24 hours to pick a rehab center that the hospital recommended. There wasn't enough time to check out the choices offered for a rehab center so I just went with the recommendation from the hospital. I choose a rehab center closest to our home.

This rehab center was also a nursing home and it was the most depressing place we had ever been. When we arrived and he got settled in his room, we truly missed the wonderful staff at the hospital and it was obvious to me why there are so many complaints about nursing homes. Chuck became so depressed and sad I couldn't bear it. He told me to take him home after the first day of being there and I was quite comfortable with that.

I called the rehab/nursing center the next day and told them I was taking him home. They were so unhappy with me and told me they couldn't understand why. I tried to explain to them how depressed he was and I needed to take him home. I chose to wait until I went back in the morning to see Chuck so that he could decide what he wanted. The next morning when I returned, he was feeling a little better and he decided with all the physical therapy he needed, that it would be best for him to stay a while longer.

Every morning, afternoon and evening, I would go to the grocery store, make him healthy food and bring it to the rehab center and sit and eat with him. We would talk and talk and he would sleep although he was usually in tremendous pain so I rarely left his side.

It would have been very easy for me to feel sorry for myself and ask all those questions of why me, why my husband, why now when we are so young and have so much to look forward to, but I could not allow myself to think that way because if I did it was all about me and not about Chuck and he was the one going through this. This is when the energy work helped me so I could center myself and find a positive outlet for my intense worry and fear.

The physical therapy was working and it helped him regain his strength but since the food was horrible, I made him three healthy meals a day. We both felt better that he was getting healthy food and food that he liked.

He was there for about ten days and then he was ready to go home. Still earlier than the rehab center liked, but he and I were ready to pack up and leave. At last, we went home.

There were so many emotions we were both feeling and yes we were still in shock. How did we handle these emotions? I must say again that I never cried so much in my life as I did during this time. Chuck was a very strong, determined, motivated and smart man who believed in himself and felt he could beat this disease. He was very proud and he didn't want anyone to know that he was going through treatments because he felt it would affect his business and his friendships. He didn't want anyone treating him different or feeling sorry for him. That's when he made the decision to only tell his immediate family for the time being and then his brothers and father a month after we told our children.

Did the diagnosis put us into a terrible state of shock, numbness and sadness? Yes, more than we could have ever imagined, but then it came time for Chuck to share his diagnosis with our children and that was the toughest part of all. It saddened us both so much, we couldn't breathe at times. Chuck was a very dynamic and outgoing person and he handled the situation with such love and tenderness. His will to live was incredibly strong and powerful and we fought together as a family to keep him alive. We all truly believed deep in our souls that he would beat this terrible disease.

My caregiving days were now in full swing and this was my new life. We were in a very strange place emotionally and physically with this disease running our lives every day. Our lives, as we knew it, stopped and now it felt as though we were two totally different people than we were before this diagnosis. It changed our relationships with each other and our children. Our family was our biggest blessing. Chuck and I were soul mates and we were very close to our children and they were all close to each other. Being diagnosed with cancer took us all by surprise and made our love for each other and our family even stronger than imaginable. This strong love shared by all of us, held us together and gave us tremendous strength to fight for his life.

Chuck's desire to keep his diagnosis a secret was harder than I thought it would be. Initially, we didn't even share the diagnosis with our children. What was the reason you might say but the answer lies only in the thoughts and wishes of the person going through this experience? Chuck felt that until he knew the type of cancer and the stage it was, he didn't want to frighten our family or make them worry more than necessary. He also didn't believe the cancer could possibly be life threatening.

This was a very difficult decision. He also felt that once others knew about the cancer, he would be treated differently by co-workers, friends and associates. It was his intention to have people talk with him, look at him and continue to have relationships with him the same as before but once they were aware of the cancer, he felt that people would tend to feel sorry for him, want to talk about it and suddenly look at him differently. This could affect his whole life and he just wanted to remain normal and positive so he could concentrate on curing himself.

I now began the intense and tedious job of finding the right doctors, healers, medicine, alternative medicine and people we could trust on our team. Day and night and relentless hours on the internet, I searched and searched for the right people who could be on our team. I called everyone I knew that might be able to refer us to any and every type of healer and doctor that could possibly help us. We were living away from our home so we did not have our wonderful community of friends and that made me feel so alone and isolated.

Although, I was crazy with my internet research, Chuck's decision was not to go on the internet himself because when you read all about the disease you felt doomed, depressed and saddened by the possible outcome. That remained my job and I was up until the early morning hours researching, blogging and trying to determine what we should do next.

What decisions had to be made and where we would go from here. I felt very good about being the one to take over the research, which I felt would free Chuck from worry and keep him motivated to live. He didn't need to read about the depressing stories he would have found on the internet.

We cried a lot and we lived with so much fear. This was a first for us and so we also felt like we had to learn everything we could about the disease and the options available. Once we put the fears and sadness on the back burner, then we could forge ahead and begin the relentless task of living, learning and healing. This was a daunting task that took years off our lives as we felt a sadness that can't be explained. We felt as though our hearts were being ripped out. This may sound negative and we weren't at all, but this is how we felt inside while trying to mask our fears and keeping smiles on our faces so we could be successful in his healing. We did expect a miracle!

Although we were inseparable and so connected, I felt that I didn't always know what he was thinking and feeling because Chuck wanted to protect me from the reality of what his treatments and the disease were doing to him. How do you understand what is going through the mind and heart of the one you love at a time like this? You don't because both of you are feeling so much pain that you don't want to bring the other person down and so you discuss only what needs to be discussed. There were times we had to be serious and open our hearts and mind to all possibilities which made us discuss things we didn't want to deal with and that was very hard. One of the times that I found the most difficult to understand what he was feeling was when he told our children that he had cancer.

Chuck felt so responsible for everything that happened in his life that sharing this with our family was breaking his heart. He felt this was worse than the actual diagnosis. He had such a difficult time knowing how hurtful and painful this would be to our family. We both agreed that telling the family was the hardest day of our lives. The reality of cancer is scary and difficult to talk about because you might have to face the worst outcome and that is too painful to bear.

Once you do realize it is real, not that we ever believed it could be the end, and we truly never faced the possibility of a serious outcome throughout this whole process, it was time to find answers and a cure. It was also time for me to remove all those fears and frightening feelings so I could be constantly positive and focused on his healing.

Our days were filled with emotions, strength, love, determination and positive thoughts.

As hard as it was to share this with our family, once it was shared and we became the unbeatable team, we bonded together and became closer than ever before. The connection that was always there between our family became stronger and the fight to win this battle was ongoing.

CHAPTER 4
WHAT'S NEXT

From this moment on the uphill battle of beating the cancer and looking for a cure began!!! Being at one of the top cancer centers in the country was the first step and we were already there. The search for the right oncologist came next. When I say finding the right oncologist, I realized it was about finding the doctor that you trust and want to have in your corner. Someone who thinks like you do and who has heart.

We began this journey of looking for the right oncologist by talking to a few different oncologists and learning everything we could about lung cancer. I researched every evening online for hours figuring out what questions to ask the oncologist. I tried to learn about all different types of treatments and every possible option we might have. I could do the research and share with Chuck what I found out but in the end, it was his decision on what direction he wanted to take. It was not my choice to force what I wanted on him but to let him evaluate his options and make his own choices on treatments. This wasn't always easy giving up that control.

There are many different beliefs when it comes to healing and medicine. Some of us believe 100% in the traditional medical world and want to follow that route of treatment while others want to follow the alternative method. There is also the option of both, some medical and some holistic. In my opinion, there is no right or wrong answer. What each person believes in their heart is right for them. When you have cancer, many times it is a matter of the quality of life you are going to have during your treatments. Does one outweigh the other? I don't know the answer because not only is it very personal but you may think one way all your life until you are faced with a life-threatening decision.

Moving forward with deciding on an oncologist, Chuck wanted someone who was vested in his survival and had the motivation to try any avenue possible to achieve that goal. Chuck began the search himself, even though the cancer center recommended a few different oncologists. Chuck then called the cancer center and asked for the best lung cancer specialist in the center. He was given a referral but he was told he could not get in to see him for a week or two but that didn't matter to Chuck, even though it was recommended he didn't wait any longer. He decided to wait. In his opinion, the time factor didn't matter but instead it was important that he wanted someone he could be comfortable with and trust with his life. This was a good decision after meeting the oncologist because he knew that this doctor was the right one for him. Chuck did connect with him and they became a team.

Chuck approached his oncologist with all heart and began the conversation letting him know the type of relationship he hoped to have with him. He shared with his oncologist that he was counting on him to get him through this cancer and give him many more years to live. This was a heart wrenching moment for both Chuck and the oncologist as the oncologist told Chuck his stage of lung cancer was treatable not curable. Chuck didn't believe him but regardless of that fact, they bonded immediately and their relationship began developing in a positive light. With that accomplished, we were onto the next task. Now all the tests began. He had so many different tests because the oncologist needed to know where the cancer had spread and what area they should attack first. There were all different types of chemotherapy which had to be decided on too.

Now, we were told that Chuck might be a good candidate for a clinical trial that would hopefully work for him and we felt good about this possibility.

Although, his oncologist and the radiologist told us again that his cancer was treatable and not curable. How did we feel about that? We didn't believe it...NO NOT possible! We believed he would be cured because there was no other possibility in our lives and so we would do whatever it took to make that happen.

The possibility of this clinical trial ended quickly when the MRI test results showed that the cancer had metastasized to the brain which made Chuck ineligible for this clinical trial.

It was now a week later and we were in the car when the phone rang. The call was from his oncologist with more bad news. It felt that from the time of his diagnosis every possible ray of hope we had was being destroyed as almost all our news was bad. We had feelings of depression and we felt that we just couldn't get a break. We continued to fight the negative feelings with positive thinking while using different energy techniques to calm us down and keep us centered and clear. We would not give up and we would fight our way through this ordeal. I was impressed with my husband because he never felt sorry for himself.

He blamed the cancer on himself because he felt that all the stress he had in his business life the last few years weakened his immune system and that was a big part of his disease. Even though we still felt sad and depressed at times, we needed to stay on track and focus on his healing.

Before we could begin the chemo treatments, the oncologist suggested we talk with the radiologist who would put a plan together for radiating the brain. Therefore, many important decisions needed to be made. Chuck was told that he could have radiation on the whole brain or use the cyber knife and only attack the specific spots they could see on the MRI. After careful thought and evaluation, he chose to have the whole brain radiated. The reason he made that decision was because after hearing there could be other spots that might not show up in the MRI, he wanted it all gone and didn't want to take any chances.

This was a difficult choice but one Chuck felt comfortable with. Realizing that during this whole time, we were still numb, devastated, sad and unsure that this was happening, but we knew we had to approach this challenge One Day at a Time, what else could we do? Otherwise, the whole process was too overwhelming to handle or think about.

Chuck was a very spiritual man and he felt a deep connection to Jesus and this was apparent when he experienced deep moments of peacefulness. His faith was miraculous during this very challenging time in our lives. I personally couldn't understand it as well as he did.

As we went back and forth to the cancer center, Chuck's empathy became so strong for other cancer patients. He would say how much it hurt him to see anyone else going through what he did.

During his time at the center in the radiation department, he was mortified when he passed by rooms filled with children's toys and wallpaper. This made him so sad to see that children were dealing with cancer and how cancer affects all people of all ages. It broke his heart. He could not imagine a child or baby going through cancer treatments. It saddened him deeply.

Chuck then began his radiation treatments which lasted for ten days, every day, to the entire head area, knee and femur bone which was the area that most of the tumor was removed from.

These ten days of radiation were long and the radiation made him extremely tired. The radiation gave him that wonderful purple color for a few weeks, which eventually disappeared.

The treatment provided some positive news and good results. We were told that the brain tumors were decreasing in size and there weren't any new signs of cancer in the brain. Finally, a ray of hope after all the bad news!

The next step for me was to continue the research work and studying and learning everything I could about lung cancer.

It was quite overwhelming researching all the websites and reading over fifteen cancer books and blogging on the internet. I can't believe how many books I read and how I surprised myself that I could comprehend and understand all the different types of healing methods that were out there. My brain was back in operation.

There was so much information on how to cure cancer. Book after book on all different ways to approach curing cancer, from food to attitude, to medical and holistic treatments. I was getting so tired researching every day and evening as I searched for the ultimate cure. I felt as though my brain was numb from exhaustion. I suddenly became this super reader and my brain comprehended more than ever before.

I became lost in the world of doctors, oncology, alternative medicine and reading about how many people say they were healed through alternative treatments, diets, etc. What do we do now and how do we make the right decisions?

I needed to be on top of my game to put together a team of doctors and nutritionists, chiropractors and healers and that is what I continued to do.

Once the radiation was complete, his oncologist was ready to jump right into the chemotherapy but after some serious thought, he decided that it was best to give Chuck a week of rest before moving ahead with the chemo. That was a great decision because of how tired he was after the ten straight days of radiation.

As his caregiver, I felt totally overwhelmed and didn't have any idea where to begin my search for alternative help.   Part of my dilemma was that we had been in the bay area for only one and a half years so I didn't have a community of friends and doctors that we knew. This was not our main residence but a temporary place at the time. I started searching the internet and I found that it was a very depressing place to get information on fourth stage lung cancer. This was a challenge for me but also an opportunity to find the strength inside of me that gave me the drive and motivation to find some healthy alternatives to these treatments. Through referrals and numerous phone calls, I found a person who did acupuncture and after conversations with this person's office, I asked my husband if he was interest in trying it.

Since Chuck had suffered with back pain for many years he was experienced with acupuncture and chiropractors and very satisfied with the results. He was going to try everything.

Where do you go to find alternative medicine besides the internet? I found it to be mostly referrals, so I called everyone I knew and talked to as many doctors, alternative medical physicians and whomever I thought that could lead me in the right direction. It was such a toss-up but what choice did I have? Remember, I was not in my home town and so I didn't have our doctors and friends to get referrals from although they were only a cell phone call away.

There were so many times in life that I thought at this age, I am losing my mind and I can't remember anything. I would think to myself, I will never be able to be my husband's caregiver because I can't do that, but I surprised myself and I surprised him too. It's amazing how we can all step up to the plate when we need to. Suddenly, I found that my mind was working so well and I could remember everything

I needed to. I read so many books, searched the internet for hours and days and months to find what I hoped would help. I made phone call after phone call and when I was told that person couldn't help me, I asked them for a referral and so it went on and on until my gut said this is the right person and then I took Chuck to meet them. This process continued for over a year.

As a caregiver, my time was limited and my resources were vast and confusing. Organizing my days, the referrals, and my husband's schedule became essential in getting through the day.

I began with a schedule that I typed out each day which consisted of the number of pills he needed to take and when he would need to take them and how much he ate at every meal, etc. I marked it off after I gave him his pills and feed him his meals. This was so helpful when we went to the oncologist's office because they asked for all this information. Organization was key!

From a learning point of view, this was a life changing experience and accepting his diagnosis was something I never fully allowed myself to do. I could only believe in his full recovery and his life being extended for many years to come and nothing and no one would change my mind. I found that soul searching became a daily task and I found I could be more patient, more loving and understanding then I had ever been, but I also found that at times I was so fearful, scared and full of anxiety and sadness. What was I to do? I couldn't allow myself to give into these emotions because I didn't have time for them and I needed to help cure my husband and be with him 24/7 while keeping him happy, feeding him positive thoughts and guiding him to the (hopefully) right team members to help us.

At this point, I was referred by a friend to look up Dr. Andrew Weil in Arizona and through that connection we were referred to a doctor in the bay area. We made an appointment to see him and he helped with some nutritional ideas along with a referral for a psychologist near our home.

This turned out to be a great referral and my husband found the psychologist to be extremely helpful. It gave Chuck a chance to discuss his feelings and fears along with his future hopes while helping him find peace within himself. He did find this peace and he was quite impressed with the psychologist, especially since he gave my husband hope. He became part of our positive team.

Another referral was a naturopathic doctor who gave us information on Germany's approach to lung cancer and the opportunity to decide if we wanted to try going there for treatments. So much to consider and so many choices. There isn't an answer to these questions because some cancer patients find treatments that work while others don't. The answer lies within you and your loved one and what you feel will be right for you.

We discussed everything together even though in the end I felt, after voicing my opinion, that his choice was the final choice because he had to feel a complete trust with his team of helpers and make decisions regarding certain vitamins, treatments, healers, etc. It was his choice because he needed to feel a connection with that person.

CHAPTER 5
DEALING WITH CANCER

C ancer is a terrible disease and dealing with the cancer treatments and their side effects is very difficult. Watching someone you love going through the emotional and physical effects of cancer tears at your heart. I found that there were so many moments I felt helpless because I had no control over the pain Chuck was enduring with his treatments.

I also felt helpless and powerless each time we were at the cancer center. I thought that he was too young at fifty-five to have to go through such painful treatments. My mind was still confused and kept telling me that this was not happening and this was not real. So many times, I wondered how were we going to endure all the emotions and physical treatments that he had to go through. Somehow, we did a great job of being strong, brave and putting on a strong front for each other. Neither of us knew what to expect and what the other person was thinking. Not knowing what to expect made us feel uneasy and scared. My stomach hurt and my insides were all in knots. I didn't want to make this worse for Chuck because I couldn't imagine how hard this must be for him already and he was trying to be so strong for me and vice versa.

Somehow I found that using energy work and talking to God was holding me together. I used many of the techniques of energy healing to keep myself focused on the good and overcome most of my fears. Chuck also learned these techniques which helped him through some of the worst moments of his treatments and again helped with the pain. We don't know what we would have done without these techniques to aid us in the on-going struggle we were facing.

On that first day in the cancer center after signing in, you sit and wait to be called back to a semi-private area with a curtain and large comfortable chair for the patient as they prepare for their infusions. Everyone at Stanford Cancer Center was fabulous. They made our experience as comfortable as they possibly could. The caring and loving nurses made it easier although at the same time my stomach was in knots trying to face this reality.

Beyond all the emotional challenges and feelings, we had to deal with the physical side effects.

After the radiation treatments, Chucks hair started to fall out. Even though expected, it was especially hard because he had a beautiful head of hair for his age and it just seemed wrong. Since it was falling out more and more, Chuck made the decision to shave his head and grow a beard. This was the first real beard he ever had. And as life would have it, the bald look was in! The timing was perfect. When our boys found out that Dad's hair was falling out and he was going to shave his head, they offered to shave their heads to make their Dad feel good. This made Chuck feel so loved. Even though he felt so honored by his sons, he told them not to do that but that he appreciated the gesture.

Another side effect was weight loss and that was starting to happen quickly. The week between radiation and chemotherapy was important for Chuck to regain his strength. This time allowed him to build up his physical and mental strength. We felt that he would have more endurance as he began the next round of treatments.

The first day of chemotherapy was scary and it turned out to be a very long day...it began at 8:30 a.m. at the cancer center because they drew his blood each time he had chemotherapy. He also had a few hours of more tests before going to the infusion room that gratefully had reclining chairs and big windows in a room filled with many cancer patients.

The staff was wonderful and the day went well. We were expecting to have a terrible time after the first day of chemotherapy but to our surprise the doctors had given Chuck steroids that he took for a few days right after chemotherapy and this gave his body the energy he needed to feel good before it crashed.

He was good for a day or two after the chemotherapy before the side effects took over. When the steroids wore off, Chuck had aches and pains throughout his body. Then nausea started and eating became a real problem.

I felt I needed to find different ways to help him enjoy food along with helping him eat nutritiously. This was a daunting task but I did find some special cookbooks for cancer * that were a tremendous help. The cancer center also had a nutritionist who gave me a list of foods that tasted good but also nutritious. They also had a handout on how to overcome some of these side effects of chemotherapy.

I never realized how much it would hurt to watch the man you love in such pain – it broke my heart every day and made me love him even more. I had no realization of what was happening in my life but instead focused totally on how to make his endurance of these painful treatment easier. For us, another obstacle was that he could not walk after the operation without crutches. He was also going to physical therapy a few times a week. This added to our already booked schedule but this was our life and we were

Deborah Pearson

living it the best we knew how. Calendars and sched-
ules were imperative to keeping all his appointments.

My heart ached and my prayers were constant.
I prayed for help every day just to make it through
one more day...just one day at a time. I constantly
needed a way to stay strong, be positive and keep
myself motivated so that I could be strong for Chuck.

Any time I needed to be away from Chuck, even
for an hour it was difficult because I wanted every
moment with him and even going to the grocery
store or running an errand seemed as though I was
gone for hours. I cried and cried and let all my emotions out while driving to the store so that I could be
strong the moment I returned home to be with him.

Our days were filled with appointments with the
physical therapist, acupuncturist, the psychologist,
naturopath and other doctor appointments so we
had little time for anything else. The worst side effects of the chemo were getting harder and harder
and he couldn't eat much. This was becoming serious because he could not keep his food down and
he was getting very weak. He was losing weight too
quickly and this was very challenging.

I was feeling at a loss again and then I remem-
bered my doctor from Arizona who I adored. She

was retired but I gave her a call for advice. It was great to reconnect with her and she directed me to a place nearby for cancer retreats. I was excited to talk with the retreat center but I was told that unless my husband could do everything on his own, we could not be part of this retreat. Since he was still on crutches and not able to be functioning by himself, we could not attend. This was a huge disappointment but we didn't give up and we kept trying everything we could think of. My emotions were overtaking my ability to stay positive sometimes as one challenge after another kept happening.

When I had made that call to the retreat house, I had a great conversation with one of the volunteers who recommended her favorite cookbook which was, *One Bite at a Time: Nourishing Recipes for People with Cancer, Survivors and their Caregivers* by Rebecca Katz and Marsha Tomassi.

The recipes were perfect for Chuck and he could start eating a little bit more than before while also adding some nutritional value to his diet which helped him gain some weight.

Another great recommendation from the nutritionist was this vitamin packed Scandi shake available at the cancer center and online. These drinks were nutritious and would also help him gain more weight.   Most cancer patients found that even with the nausea they could drink them. The nutritionist who suggested them also suggested that we add honey, yogurt, bananas, ice cream and all sorts of nutritional and not so nutritional foods which brought the caloric intake to 1,000 calories a shake. At last, something he could drink. This was true because he was drinking three a day which was wonderful because eating solids were impossible. These Scandi shakes were working because he started gaining weight and feeling better.

Even though we did get through some of these difficult times, I felt like I wanted to just sit and cry a lot because I was so tired and emotionally drained. I couldn't believe my heart could hurt so much. As much as I didn't want to, I found myself crying in front of him and breaking down. I became so frustrated, tired and angry and totally exhausted. I tried to keep these emotions to a minimum and continued to search within for the strength to go on.

⊱ ⊰

We felt very fortunate to encounter some very inspiring times and one that helped us happened at the cancer center when Chuck was walking into the room for his CT Scan. He told me that he felt Jesus put his hand on his shoulder which gave him such a wonderful sensation of peace. Chuck has experienced so many moments when he felt Jesus right by his side and many times during meditation he could see Jesus in this beautiful lush meadow. Chuck said he didn't want to leave this place he was in when meditating because it was so beautiful and loving.

We were married 33 years when he was diagnosed. Through those years we became so connected that we could feel one another's emotions and we could also read each other's mind. I know he could see the pain I was feeling which made him try so hard to keep his pain from me.

This was so hard for him because his pain was extremely overwhelming. His body was always aching, tired and nauseous during and after his treatments.

We realized that we needed to have a hospital bed in our living room because he was having trouble walking up the stairs to the master bedroom. I found myself sitting on his hospital bed every day in the morning and night. I would read motivational books and wellness cards to him which would inspire him and help him find hope when he was down.

With all these outside sources helping us nothing could compare to the love our children had for their Dad. The love pouring out of our children and their wives was so amazing and through this tough time our family became his best motivating support. Without their love and support, I could not have had the energy, motivation and constant positive attitude that I felt.

When Chuck decided not to share his cancer with anyone outside our family, it felt like torture because I felt that there were times that I needed the support of friends. During these times when I felt sorry for myself, I realized I had to take my feelings out of the situation and I understood that it was his decision and this was not about me but about us together fighting this battle.

This was such a personal decision and one that I needed to respect even when it was so difficult. In the end, it was a good decision because since we were living away from our friends and family we had each other and this time we had together became a very cherished time in our lives.

We had our difficult moments and discussions about him eating enough, about his pain management and worst of all it was so hard to talk about what I should do if he didn't make it. I couldn't bear the thought and so I didn't allow myself the acknowledgement of that possibility. This made it very hard for Chuck to talk to me and tell me what he needed to because frankly, I didn't let him. The times were far and few between but we did have some of those discussions, mostly about business and that he wanted me to be happy. We were enduring so much together and separately, that we didn't know how to express our fears openly. We became inseparable and our love was completely unconditional. It wasn't all bliss as I pushed him to get better and keep fighting even when he was so tired and didn't want to keep fighting anymore because of the pain.

We had a fabulous thirty-four years of marriage and four years of dating together and our marriage was one of the best parts of my life. Who knew it could be better and so unconditionally full of love and acceptance of each other. We shared so many memories, thoughts, feelings that were not the easiest things to share during our marriage, but this crisis helped us be more open. This revelation makes me want to shout to the world, love your partner, accept that person for whom they are and give all the love you can every day because no one can predict tomorrow.

Sometimes in life when you think this is more than you can handle and you're devastated, God sends you an angel to give you hope and a reason to keep believing and the strength to keep fighting.

One of our weaker moments was when we were both having a hard time emotionally but then while we were at the cancer center one day, we needed to take the elevator down to X-rays and as the elevator opened a man pushing a cart of supplies said he would move over so we could fit in the elevator with Chuck's wheelchair. We told the gentleman we would just take the next elevator but he insisted we get in. This stranger who came out of nowhere, began to tell us that he had fourth stage liver cancer and was doing very well and that he was in remission. It was as though he knew what we were going through and he wanted to give us hope. This brightened our day and we talked about it for a long time. Why would he randomly tell us that without knowing us or talking to us? We congratulated him and thanked God for those words of encouragement. We both felt this man was our angel coming to tell us to keep the faith and to believe that we will be okay.

Chuck's energy and attitude had been up and down throughout these treatments which was to be expected. For him, part of keeping the positive attitude and lifestyle we had, was for us to go out as often as physically possible. He liked being out of the house. We did things like driving around the city, going out to lunch and dinner whenever possible, if he didn't have an appetite it didn't matter because that pushed him to feel better and normal and not lay in the hospital bed all day and evening. We needed to find things to motivate us and keep us busy.

At the beginning when we were in such a state of numbness and denial, the psychologist suggested that we ask our family to write down what inspires each one of us so we could share that with Chuck. Everyone in our family including myself wrote him a letter sharing our feelings for him and our love and support. I asked my family to call me and record their inspirations on a voice recorder so Chuck could take this with him during his chemotherapy sessions.

How encouraging and positive an idea this was. It made him feel so good and he was so proud of his children and their spouses. Their incredible stories touched his heart in a way that can't be put into words. Everyone's letter was so unique, loving and inspiring. We were so touched by their stories and their love that poured out of them.

This was the best idea for our family and it touched our hearts. It also gave our children the opportunity to share from their hearts and connect in a totally different way with their father. This was one of the best suggestions ever! Chuck felt so supported and loved by his family and this gave him the will to keep fighting for his life.

"ONE DAY AT A TIME" became our motto because the overwhelming process of the treatments, research, appointments and challenging side effects from the chemo became so hard to manage that I needed to feel less overwhelmed and by thinking about one day at a time life became more manageable.

Every time I became overwhelmed and over worked, I told myself over and over, One Day at a Time. This idea sure changes how I was thinking, because I didn't concentrate on future events and what will happen next but instead I tried to enjoy every day and every moment of that day as though it were the last.

We needed to laugh more and talk about the things that made us happy so we could focus on the good in life. We celebrated all events, both big and small. Times as simple as when he could eat a meal, we celebrated together. The little things in life became huge and became an important milestone in his healing.

Since this experience was so new to us, and even though I read numerous books, it was hard for anyone to tell you what to expect and we felt on our own in many ways. I put together a schedule but I learned that when exhaustion overtakes you, you just go with it, relax, sleep, rest so you have the energy to keep up with the pace of everything going on. Easier said than done.

Every day was consumed with taking X-rays, doctor appointments, physical therapy, reading motivational books and watching movies like "The Secret" or movies that made us laugh and think positive all while enduring the side effects of chemo and the dry throat, achy body, nausea and constipation.

It was hard to find a way to help ourselves work through this and since I didn't have the time to call my children every day and give them all the updates, I would send out an email once a week with all the details of everything that was happening. This helped them stay connected with us when I was either too tired or didn't have any alone time to chat with them. That may sound strange that I didn't have time to call my own children but so many days were filled with appointments and physical therapy and preparing certain types of food and sitting with him, helping him endure the pain that by the time

I could have some down time, it was very late and I was exhausted. The days just went so fast.

Some days were good and everything was moving in the right direction and other days were a nightmare with the pain, aching, not eating, feeling nauseous. Life was totally unpredictable and going with the flow was a new way of life for me since I am the organized, everything in its place type of person. We had so many lessons to learn and so much growing to do while trying to keep the faith.

Research consumed much of my time as I read books and called around for other ideas to find a cure. I learned a lot about myself and about this disease that has raptured his body. The hardest part for me now was watching him suffer because he couldn't walk without crutches and the side effects were devastating. Also, the emotional toll was more than I realized because when you are in the throes of being a caregiver, you just keep going and nothing stops you and trying to find time to rest is almost impossible. Sleep is hard to get so meditating and praying were constant.

We did try many avenues of treatments hoping for that cure while keeping our thoughts focused only on healing and surviving.

Between the difficulty of physical therapy and the pain medicine, not being able to eat most of the time along with so many more side effects from the chemo, he still had a great attitude and he was grateful for what he had. He felt so blessed that we had our wonderful family and a good life.

When it came to managing the pain medication it was very difficult. Some of the medications were so strong and made him so cranky, so what were our choices? At one point, he was on morphine for the pain but it made him sleep all day and all evening so Chuck decided to call his doctor and tell him that this was not going to work because he wanted to live his life not to be sleeping through it. Although, he still needed strong meds he could use a medication that didn't make him sleep all day or make him so cranky. The fact that he needed crutches to walk made it even more difficult and depressing at times.

When Chuck meditated, he could relieve a lot of the pain and he felt emotionally better. His meditations and energy work helped him deal with his pain, his fears and emotions.

We talked about focusing on what we appreciated about life and each other. We reminisced about all our good times and funny memories. As we shared those stories and memories with each other it strengthened us and kept us connected. We knew that our thoughts created our life and so we were determined not to let this horrific disease ruin the time we had together. Of course, there were many moments when we both were sad and angry and frustrated and sometimes we picked it out on each other and our family. We tried to be aware of those times because they would just come over us, but we tried very hard to control those thoughts and focus on the good.

One of his doctors advised Chuck and myself to journal every day about what we wanted in life and it helped to write about our feelings. It helped us understand many of the emotions we were experiencing.

That was very hard for Chuck especially when he was in a lot of pain, which was often during all the chemo treatments and the operation on his right femur bone created so much pain. Physical therapy was also very painful. He tried swim therapy sessions a few times a week to help with his leg and that became a real challenge for Chuck. It wore him out and he found that his energy level was so low and his appetite decreased so much that he now was 50 pounds thinner. He also had the chills a lot and it was hard keeping him warm, even with a heating blanket. Another side effect of the chemo affected his teeth and he needed a root canal while also dealing with pain everywhere else in his body. It was never-ending!!! He became weak from all the treatments and had fallen a few times too. The good thing was that when he had fallen we were home and he didn't get hurt.

Blood transfusions were a common occurrence now which gave him strength and made him feel better.

It is so easy to take our physical being for granted until suddenly you are incapacitated in some way and then life changes and you suddenly have this unbelievable appreciation for health. Just walking at the beach or holding hands while you're walking down the street wasn't possible anymore. We couldn't go anywhere, even visiting family without a wheelchair or crutches and a place to make his Scandi shake. There were so many new challenges to make part of our daily routine but we did it.

When we went out to dinner, I would drop him off in the front of the restaurant, park and then after dinner get the car and pick him up. That doesn't seem like much, but when you consider this is just one little area that is new and different along with everything else you're doing, it can become over-whelming. But more importantly, it weighs on your heart and emotions because the emotions I was feeling were so strong and I kept them suppressed most of the time.

It would be so easy to get caught up in the negative emotions of feeling sorry for myself and being sad. Believe me, I was many times and I found that I had to let myself go through my pity party and then pick myself up and focus only on what I appreciated and how much I loved him and wanted to be there with him. Once I started changing my thoughts, life was so much better even in the worst of circumstances.

With each MRI, CT or PET Scan there was good news but also bad news. We never felt that we didn't have one without the other. The oncologist would tell us that the area around the lungs was shrinking but the pelvic area was getting larger. This was when it was especially hard to stay positive and not feel defeated from all the constant bad news. We felt discouraged and sad from these results and we knew when we needed to meditate and change our thoughts again because we went back and forth between being determined, strong and sad and discouraged. It was a constant yoyo effect on our emotions. I feel we were positive most of the time and tried very hard to keep healing as the end goal!

When I researched all the alternative methods of treatment, which were overwhelming at best, then decisions had to be made. Going to Mexico or Germany for other types of treatments or using conventional methods, how do you decide? I was feeling so lost with all possibilities and what and who to believe. I guess after listening to everything and everyone's different opinions and stories, all the alternative treatments, conventional doctors, Chinese medical practices, acupuncture specialists, naturopaths you come to the point where you know must evaluate your options and follow your heart but more importantly, listen to the wishes of the cancer patient. Sometimes leaving it up to the person going through it can be very hard if he believes one way and you believe a different way.

CHAPTER 6
REMISSION
"A MONUMENTAL DAY"

Today was April 15th, 2008 (Tax Day!) and we had an appointment with Chuck's oncologist. Chuck had been on a trial drug for a few months now but when we went to see his oncologist today, he informed us that none of the treatments were working anymore. He told Chuck that after nine months of radiation, chemotherapy and the chemo trial that we would need to call hospice and be sure everything was in order because there wasn't much time left.

You can imagine our shock, we both just froze and looked at each other for a minute and then quickly Chuck responded, **"Doctor, I am not going to die yet, I have lots more to do and it's not my time. He said, this is not up to us and I know that God is not ready for me. This is between me and my God!"** To the shock of his oncologist, Chuck said, "Tell me doc, what would you do if this was you?" The look on the doctor's face was priceless. He was stunned that Chuck could relate this way to him. The best part is that there was a special connection between Chuck and his oncologist. Chuck made sure of deeply connecting with his doctor on the first day they met. He told me that he was going to be sure his doctor didn't think of him as a number, but as someone to which he was emotionally connected. It worked because the two of them did have a connection, as hard as that was for his doctor.

After the initial shock of this sad news and discussions on finding something else to keep him alive, his oncologist told Chuck there was another drug which was in pill form called Tarceva and it was worth trying. The oncologist felt that it wasn't as strong a drug as his other chemo, but it had worked for some patients. Decision made… we were ready to try this drug.

At the diagnosis time, we were told Chuck had three months to live which none of us believed. We couldn't even wrap our heads around that idea and so we didn't accept the diagnosis then and we didn't accept it now.

This was a real blow to our family because Chuck was gaining weight, almost walking without crutches, had less pain and then this! Why the constant challenge? How much more can we deal with?

Hearing this news was another shock to our system, we couldn't even talk so we went home and just stayed in each other's arms all night. While we were lying in bed that night, Chuck looked at me and said, "I know I am not going to die yet, I feel as though God is healing me and I am going to be okay." He was so positive and felt so sure of himself. He was totally confident and knew in his heart he had more time. He had this inner sense of knowing that this was not his time and he was right all along, so far.

I personally was a mixture of emotions and between the fear and the sadness, I finally gave in to crying all night long. I just wanted to be in his arms all day and night and never move. I felt the pain, the hurt, the deep sadness in my heart and I let myself have this experience for a little while. Then I realized I couldn't be this negative anymore. I needed to pick myself up and get back into believing he was going to make it. We were going to survive this! We had to! I was using all the techniques that my dear friend, Barbara Mahaffey, taught me. She is a Holistic Energy Psychologist and we have known each other for over thirty years. She practices Energy Awareness and uses techniques and tools that keep you centered. These techniques help you deal with the pain and stress so it doesn't take over your life. These exercises and tools worked so we used them as much as possible.

The Next Day: April 16, 2008

This is almost impossible to believe and I wouldn't believe it if I hadn't witnessed it with my own eyes but the next morning when Chuck woke up, he looked better, felt better and the healing began. He started eating more for the next few weeks and life changed for the better. He started living a more normal and happier life. His hair started growing back and he had more energy. He even became stronger and able to walk better. At one point, he was almost able to walk without the crutches. The physical therapy was working now too. This was so drastic and so exciting. We were relieved that everything was improving.

We went to dinner and we were back to traveling to see our children. During all these treatments, Chuck would still fly for business and that was quite a challenge. From going through the airport with a wheelchair and having the metal in his leg meant he was always pulled aside and needed to go through a special type of security screening. This took more time and was painful for him. Since this was so painful, we had to medicate appropriately for flying and while keeping him coherent and hopefully this would help the pain. He struggled to have enough strength to just get into a seat on the plane. He was such a trooper and he still wanted to fly and travel even though it was such a challenge. He did it so well because he was so determined to live his life fully.

Finally, the time had come when we could see the light at the end of the tunnel...Yay! The pain was subsiding and he was taking less medication. This felt like the miracle we prayed for. It was happening and Chuck was in remission. We were so incredibly happy and relieved. This was amazing and we truly appreciated everyone on our team who helped us get here, especially and most importantly our family.

During all those treatments, his voice became hoarse and softer which was so unlike Chuck because he had a voice that was so powerful you could hear him across the room. He was told by so many people that he could have been an announcer or speaker because of the power in his voice.

This incredible feeling of being in remission made him so happy. It was wonderful for me to see a smile on his face and enthusiasm in his voice. We even talked about traveling out of the country again. We realized our passports were expiring and so we renewed them. When we looked at the pictures on our passports, we laughed so hard because with his bald head and weight loss he looked like a criminal. This was so funny to us and it felt so good to laugh like this again.

Our children were very happy and ready to have their Dad back again in their lives without all the everyday challenges of this disease. We were all feeling positive and uplifted. We were ready to put the past behind us and move forward. We were thrilled to have our Chuck back!!!! This miracle wasn't perfect and he was still healing so he was still experiencing some pain. All the side effects of the treatments stayed in his body for a long time even though his body was trying to slowly recover.

There was nothing in our opinion, like cancer or I am sure any other serious illness to show you how important your health is. Words can't describe the affect disease has on your mind and your body. More than that, it changes your whole attitude about health and what is important in life. Without your health, life is so much harder and it is so easy to take your health for granted.

Chuck loved to cook and he started helping me in the kitchen again, cooking some of his favorite meals and creating some of his own recipes too.

He could sit up and eat dinner at the table with me now. This wasn't as easy before because most of the time he would lay in his hospital bed and eat a little bit and sitting up in the chair had also been so painful.

Cancer treatments are a catch twenty-two – the treatments are sometimes worse than the disease and they kill all the good and bad cells in your body so how do you survive these treatments and side effects? You're doomed if you do and doomed if you don't.

Although, we always felt he could beat this or at least be in remission for a long time, we now saw the reality of our beliefs. Chuck could feel the positive transformation in his body every day since he was told to call hospice. Not to say that every day since he was told it was over, was great because it wasn't. We still had good days and bad days. Some days we were so positive and he could feel his body healing. Then there were other days he woke up feeling fearful, weak and mentally and emotionally scared to death. Although we knew this was normal, you don't think about that when you are going through it. You can lose hope for a day until you realize that will destroy you so you change your thoughts and you continue to fight for your survival.

After watching him get so weak where he could barely make it to the bathroom without having the chills, severe aching, losing weight, losing his voice, being tired and I could go on and on about all the side effects of his treatments. There was now this ray of hope that was bringing joy and light back into our lives.

About ten days after his terminal diagnosis along with this new chemotherapy pill, Chuck walked with only one crutch instead of two. For the first time in a year, he could hold my hand and walk across the street with me. That may sound unimportant but it meant the world to us. There were so many little things we couldn't do anymore and we missed them so much that when one little thing like holding hands was possible, we were both elated. Laughter filled our lives again and our spirits were lifted. We went out to dinner again and we truly began enjoying all the simple things in life.

We drove to the beach one day and the weather was terribly cold and windy so we sat in the car and opened the windows and just talked. We talked about how energy work was helping and what our goals were for the future and how much we still wanted to do in our lives.

We reminisced about some of the worst times we had when he couldn't even dress himself or stand up for any length of time. He would get so cold inside and feel so weak. Nothing would warm him up except sometimes the heating blankets would help.

So much has changed since starting on the Tarceva. He is now able to dress himself, eat and although it was slowly getting back to some sense of normalcy, it was working. He was improving, though intermittently. He was gaining weight and getting stronger but he still had some pain and he continued to take some of his pain medication.

He had gained eight pounds in two weeks and his blood work looked better. His oncologist was happier too, which made Chuck more confident. It was now June of 2008 and Chuck was walking upstairs without crutches and had gained nineteen pounds since April. Twice a week he still had physical therapy and that seemed to help him quite a bit. Meditation and energy work were an everyday occurrence which helped us start our day in good spirits. We needed that. There were days now that Chuck didn't even take a pain pill. We could see the improvements happening in every area and there was a steady change for the better.

Surprisingly, he drove alone by the end of June. Chuck was feeling so much better we decided to take a family vacation together. Although he was tired a lot, he was eating and getting around easier. We were at the beach on vacation so he did need to stay away from the sun because of the chemotherapy that he had.

This was a great week. Chuck could walk around during the Art Festival and we even had family visit us. Our days were busy again and maybe at times we overdid it, so when we came back to the house after a day out, he was very tired and slept for a few hours.

In July, we returned to the oncologists office for a checkup and he said that Chuck's blood work was great and he would only need to see him every 6-8 weeks now. His oncologist even felt that Chuck surprised him when he went into remission. He told Chuck that statistics say he shouldn't be alive but every so often there is that one in 100th person that doesn't follow statistics. Today, Chuck was that One!!!

It is uncanny how life brings people to you that help you through the tough times. We still had to go to the Cancer center and one afternoon we experienced another enlightening story. While we were sitting in the cancer center, Chuck met a very nice lady who shared with him her story on how she was also told to call hospice five years ago. Today she was still around in remission from colon cancer. He told her not to give up and keep fighting and that he was very happy for her. These are the moments that you know an angel is being sent to help you and give you hope.

Today was July 17, 2008 and thirty-eight years ago we had gone on our first date. Life goes by so fast. We could finally celebrate and truly enjoy these days together.

Each day was a blessing because you never know what tomorrow will bring. Did I speak too soon because the next day was scary. When he woke up his leg and ankle were swollen. We surmised that this was because of all the walking he did without his crutches for the last two months. The swelling created some new challenges again, but we dealt with it. He just needed to elevate his legs. Fear immediately set in and he found that his emotions were so hard to control when something discouraging happened. Of course, the challenges did affect his moods. I am sure between the cancer, the treatments, the pain medication that even though he was doing very well, after all he had been through, he would get depressed when something scared him.

August 1, 2008

Today was one of Chuck's happiest days because his first granddaughter was born. Since that fateful day when Chuck was diagnosed I hadn't seen much joy left in his heart but today he was beaming. He talked about how much he wanted grandchildren and he couldn't wait to be a grandparent. His dream came true today and I could feel his love and excitement radiating when he first met her.

During that week Chuck was so happy. Soon after her birth, we had more good news. Our second son and his wife were pregnant and going to have a baby in March. We cried with joy and felt such happiness in our hearts. This was a great week!

It was about two weeks later and Chuck's legs were swelling again. This caused us to feel nervous and a bit scared again.

August 12

We had another appointment with his oncologist and Chuck's blood work was still good. The pain in his legs was on and off so he was also on and off with the pain meds. This was still a constant challenge. When you are feeling, better and trying to wean yourself off these heavy medications, it is still important to keep enough medication in your system so that when the pain returns you don't start from scratch.

September 8

It was our 34th anniversary on August 30th and we vacationed in Carmel, CA. We laughed and had a great time. He was feeling better and his leg was better too.

September 10

Chuck went to the barber shop today for a haircut. Yes, that means his hair had grown back too. After that, he went for a CT Scan and the technician could see the worry in Chuck's face again. He told him that the choice of living was not up to the doctors but up to him. His words of encouragement helped Chuck bring back his positive attitude again. His overall pain was better and he was on Advil instead of the heavy pain meds.

His oncologist called about the brain scan and although there were small spots the full results were not back yet. So far, he did not have any new cancer and some of the smaller spots were gone. Unfortunately, the lung tumor grew from 2 centimeters to 4. During this whole process, we still had so many emotional ups and downs. It was a constant yoyo effect and I held up well, although I was a bit worried.

September 13

We had a date. We went to a nice French restaurant and reminisced about our trips and how much fun we had. Chuck ate most of his dinner and his leg pain was minor. This was great because he still only needed Advil to take the pain away. All the difficult times seemed so unimportant and instead we have been focusing on our happy times and how much in love we were.

September 25

Something was changing and Chuck had been vomiting for the last two weeks which was accompanied by extreme nausea. We traveled for a few days with our dear friends but Chuck was beginning to feel tired again and nauseous. He had to go back on some pain meds, but not every day.   He was also still vomiting now and then. Suddenly, he had a hard time holding his dinner down which made him feel very depressed.

September 26

Chuck had been taken off the Tarceva as of September 12th because the CT Scan showed the tumor on his lung was growing.   He wasn't taking any medication for a while but decided, against his oncologists opinion, to start this new clinical trial that he heard about. The reason the oncologist didn't want him to be part of the clinical trial was because he didn't feel Chuck had the physical strength to handle it. Chuck was adamant that he couldn't give up and needed to keep fighting for his life and so he made the decision to start this new trial.

September 29

We spent six and a half hours at the cancer center today. Chuck could not keep food down all day so his oncologist sent him for a Chest X-ray and blood work. He was feeling very tired and he was anemic now too. He has been having sweats and stomach pains. The weight issue is back and he is losing more weight again.

October 1

We realized today that he now had this lump on his shoulder that had never been there before. It was very large and swollen. As you can imagine, this caused us both to start worrying and so I called to make an appointment with the oncologist. This was scaring both of us.

October 9 – 12

His oncologist decided to schedule a CT Scan for Chuck to see why he had this large growth on his shoulder. The result from this scan was seriously upsetting. This was a new tumor and he also had other new tumors that had grown in different areas as well.

This is what I mean by the ups and downs because the next few days he was feeling much better again.

One day good, one day bad. Things were constantly changing and now sleeping was becoming difficult for him. He was experiencing lots of pain in his stomach and he started with dry heaves. Eating was also a problem now and the pain was getting worse.

October 14

Today was a tough day at the oncologist's office. The clinical trial was brought up again and his oncologist was totally against Chuck going on this trial. He felt Chuck was too weak to handle it. He told Chuck they were out of options and he didn't know of anything else that would help him. Chuck didn't agree because he was fighting to survive with every fiber of his being. He decided he wanted to go on the clinical trial to see if he could be healed. For Chuck to start this trial, he needed to have many tests done beforehand. He was getting weaker every day. His oncologist told Chuck to be prepared for the worst and that he was not going to get better. This news was so devastating. We were in remission and feeling so good for a while, how could this be? We still didn't believe this because we could not accept Chuck not being with us. We still believed he could beat it.

I didn't just pray anymore, I begged God to heal him. I could not imagine life without Chuck. I'm sorry, but I am not accepting anything but survival. My family being an incredible source of strength for us stayed positive and hopeful through this whole ordeal. I could not accept losing Chuck and therefore I could not relay to my family how sick he was because I didn't see how sick he was getting or accept it. I could not allow my mind to even think he wasn't going to survive. I didn't believe he could be dying even though when looking back it was obvious. I just couldn't face that possibility. We loved him so much that we could not fathom life without Chuck.

October 16 - 25

Another reason I could not believe I could lose him was because again within the next few days, Chuck had an endoscopy and there was good news. No cancer in his stomach. He did have some ulcerations and irritation but no cancer. We took every little bit of good news as a ray of hope. The next day was better and we went shopping together. Chuck was eating again and in less pain. He still had some vomiting issues and his feet were a little swollen.

Saturday on October 25th, Chuck had lots of energy and enthusiasm. He was feeling good; we went out to breakfast and he held everything down. We just didn't know what to think at this point because he was feeling better again. He also had a rash for a week but that disappeared too. He is doing well and drinking 4-6 bottles of water which is another good sign. We were feeling positive and happy because he had more energy and he could eat out again. Things were looking up!

October 28 – November 25

The experience with the clinical trial was extremely difficult. It caused severe weakness and he wasn't handling it well at all. He was getting worse. When we spoke with the oncologist, he told us that Chuck would probably get weaker each week now and there was nothing else he could do. We still didn't believe him. Why would we, he was going to beat this cancer! The reality was that Chuck was taking a turn for the worse as he started losing weight and getting very weak. At this point, it made it almost impossible for Chuck to get out of bed. This sounds terrible and it was terrible. That is why it was hard to believe that we were still experiencing good and bad days. The biggest challenge was his physical body was weak one day and the next day he would regain some strength. Mornings seemed good and holding down food was better one day but not the next.

We are both experiencing immense feelings. We cry, we talk, we laugh, we feel frozen in time. We share our thoughts and feelings and talk about what a wonderful life we have had together as we spend every moment of every day together.

Chuck told me that if and only if something were to happen to him, he was a very lucky man. He had a wonderful life and fabulous children and a great wife. He felt he lived his life to the fullest. I couldn't listen to that kind of talk because it made me so sad and so frightened. I was honored he felt that way and happy he had no regrets, but I didn't want to hear these words that scared me deep in my soul.

Since he was having all these ups and downs again, Chuck was now back downstairs in the hospital bed because the steps to our bedroom were too hard to climb. He was getting weaker and feeling groggy sometimes even when on light medication.

On Monday November 24th, I took Chuck to a new doctor who infused him with a nutritional IV in hopes that this would boost his immune system. Chuck didn't handle it well and the doctor told me that Chuck was not doing well and he couldn't help him. I still did not believe this was hopeless. I was going to keep fighting for his life. Even though, he was getting weaker and eating and drinking was becoming impossible.

CHAPTER 7

THE LAST FEW DAYS

Tuesday, November 25

Chuck woke up feeling very weak. I called the oncologist and asked if Chuck could please come in and be hooked up to a nutritional IV. He was having a hard time drinking water except when using a teaspoon or a dropper and he didn't look good at all.

I noticed that the tumor on his neck was growing fast but I thought if I could get food and water in him that he would live and get better.

His oncologist did call me back and he said to please bring Chuck in. We arrived at the cancer center and they began an IV immediately and he was in great pain. The oncologist came into the room and when I saw the look on his face, I suddenly knew that this was going to be a horrible day. I was shaking and scared and still fighting for his life. We were both told together that this was the end and that we needed to call our family. The oncologist asked Chuck what he wanted to do, stay at the hospital or go home? Chuck said, "I want to stay here and get better".

I truly believed in miracles and I kept thinking that Chuck would be one of those miracles and we would be going home.

I called our children and they all arrived within a day. Chuck was then transferred from the cancer center over to the hospital that afternoon. He was beginning to lose his ability to talk and the pain was becoming unbearable.

This first night in the hospital was extremely tough. I stayed up all night with him while he was trying to sleep. His pain was so unbearable and none of the medications were working.

Our family was together now and we were all praying and crying but still hoping. There is no such word in our vocabulary as giving up and we didn't until the very end. How do you say good-bye to the one you love – how do you? I couldn't. The next few days were very difficult and Chuck could not talk to us but he could communicate through his eyes and through his inner voice. I could hear his voice inside my head without him having to speak out loud.

Thursday, November 27

Today was Thanksgiving and we were all together in the hospital with Chuck. That evening while I was sleeping in the hospital cot right next to him, I heard his voice calling my name and asking me to come over to his bed. He could not speak so I knew he was talking to me with his mind. I got off my cot and walked over to his bed which was only 4 steps away. When I looked in his eyes and sat on his bed, I knew that I needed to let go. My son told me that his Dad would not go until I told him it was okay. I couldn't imagine saying it was okay until this moment. I sat on his bed in total shock and exhaustion but I said to Chuck, "I love you with all my heart and I don't want to tell you this but I think for your sake I need to let you go." I let him know that it was okay with me and that I loved him so much. I would be missing him more than I could imagine. I sat there and held his hand for a very long time.

He was in so much pain and I knew in my heart this wasn't right for him anymore to hold on when he was so ill. We all told Chuck it was okay to go.

I did ask him to please hang on a little longer as I didn't want to lose him on Thanksgiving Day. I knew with his will and strength he would try and hang on throughout the day.

He was a fighter and he managed to live through Thanksgiving.

Friday and Saturday, November 28 and 29

Today was a very tough day in the hospital because Chuck was in and out of consciousness all day. It was sometime in the afternoon that most of my family went to the cafeteria for food, but my daughter was still in the room.

I went into the bathroom which was in the same room and when I came out I felt this incredible chill. The room was cold and it felt so strange. I looked at my daughter and asked her what was happening and she said something is wrong. I walked over to Chuck's bed. I could see he was still breathing but he wasn't there. I knew his soul had left his body but his body was still alive. It was the most unusual, cold and bizarre feeling I have ever experienced.

I felt his soul was no longer in his body, yet he was still alive. The rest of my family came back into the room and noticed immediately that the room was cold. They also said Dad was alive but not there. We all felt that his soul had left his body.

I didn't want to go over to his bed because it felt so strange and I didn't know who was lying in the bed, but it wasn't the Chuck I knew.

It took me a few minutes before I could walk over to him. I asked him to please come back into his body. We all waited and it seemed like forever, but I think it was only a matter of minutes and then we could all feel him come back into his body. The room felt normal and warm again and we could see he was back.

When our bodies could no longer sustain life, our soul leaves. I always believed that our souls live on but our bodies can't live without our souls. It was such a unique and unusual feeling to see this happen to my husband.

This happened around 5:30 P.M. on Friday and at 6:20 after Chuck returned to his body for a while, his body did succumb to this horrible disease and he left us for a better place.

I know that he is with Jesus and I truly believe he is happy and free from all the physical and emotional pain. The pain is now with us and we are left behind to deal with our grief and our loss. None of us could believe that he was truly gone. We truly believed that he would get better and be with us for many more years. The shock was overwhelming and we were not ready for a world without Chuck. I can't put into words my feelings because I felt so devastated and exhausted. We couldn't believe he was gone….it wasn't possible. I felt that I couldn't make him live longer, even after everything we tried and these thoughts stayed with me for a very long time.

CHAPTER 8
WHAT NOW?

It was the evening of November 28th. Today had been the worst day of our lives and this day would be etched in our hearts forever.

How do you say good-bye to the one you love? To your husband, your dad, your brother, your son? There are no words to explain this loss. I looked at him one last time and even though I felt this coldness because he was no longer there in his body, I still didn't want to leave that hospital room. I was so numb and so overwhelmed with grief that I just walked out of the room into the room down the hall where they kept us waiting forever, so it seemed. We had to wait to sign papers before we could leave and we were all just beside ourselves with grief.

Getting into the car to drive home from the hospital was like moving a brick wall since I could barely move my body. I felt stuck in time and I felt this strong heaviness come over me. Driving home from the hospital was a blur and then I pulled into the driveway alone without Chuck. This alone feeling was so overpowering that I thought I would die. I had lost my soul mate, my partner and our family would never be the same.

I hesitate as I put my hand on the door handle knowing what lurks inside the door– emptiness, sadness, a broken heart and a life without my love. I felt that my heart will never be repaired and never heal. How could it when the pain was so deep. The next step was to walk through that door and begin the next journey of my life. There were so many steps ahead of me and none of which I could imagine, understand or anticipate. After all, I was just beginning the grieving process.

It's late, I haven't slept in days and now I walk into my bedroom. By this time the pain is so unbearable that I keel over in tears as I experience my broken heart. Is it possible that I could feel pain so deep in my soul? Well, I guess the answer is yes because I am feeling it, aren't I? As I looked around the room and saw everything in its place just like it was when I left, I felt an overwhelming need to run away and pretend this wasn't happening.

I started thinking to myself, will I be able to live through this or will I die from a broken heart? I know the human body can endure so much, but can I endure this pain? I didn't think so then.

I truly at that moment, wanted to die so I could be with him. Dying would be easier than to keep enduring this pain and living without my love.

My oldest son mentioned how strange it was to see all Dad's stuff on the desk and all his belongings but no Dad. These are feelings you can't imagine having when you have never experienced a loss before and it felt like a slap in the face when the reality that he was gone hit us.

The material things in life remain but the person you love is gone. This was such a strange sensation. And although we value life more, the reality of death hit us like a ton of bricks.

The first night was surreal and I woke up in the middle of the night screaming. This just couldn't be real and I was so numb and in shock. Even though I was so lucky to be comforted by my children and to have them all around me, our pain as a family was incomprehensible.

We were all traumatized and in shock that he had died at only 56 years old because we expected him to be with us for a very long time. I think we can all say this about a lot of people but if you knew Chuck and how dynamic he was and so full of life, it just wasn't possible. His passing was a shock to everyone he knew. Chuck had a presence that illuminated a room when he walked in and he was the last person you would ever have expected to get cancer and die so young.

Since I never believed in my heart that Chuck would leave us, we didn't do anything in planning for a funeral. To make this even harder, we had to find a funeral home, a cemetery and take care of all the services within a few days. Chuck wanted to be buried somewhere close to Loyola Marymount where our children went to college and so with family referrals we decided on a cemetery in Culver City. He did not want to be buried in the ground or cremated so we chose the community mausoleum. And so, the process began.

The first step was going to the funeral home which was heart wrenching and the beginning of the first real dose of reality. The funeral director starting asking so many questions but I was still numb and in shock and didn't even know how to answer as I sat there speechless. Thank God for my children who helped me get through this whole process even though their grief was just as intense, they were strong enough to help me make these decisions.

The reality of his death was still not real for any of us and so we barely moved along doing what needed to be done. I think that numbness temporarily protects you from completely losing it every minute of every day. I found that just the mention of his name was difficult at best but to then deal with all the arrangements was so painful and exhausting.

For us we had a traditional viewing and mass with a reception that followed. I can't get it out of my mind when I walked into the funeral home and walked over to the room where Chuck was laid to rest. I stood there at the door and saw his name on the door of the room I was about to enter. I felt as though someone was putting a sword through my heart and I wanted to just fall and cry or scream at the top of my lungs in pain. I couldn't breathe for a moment and don't remember too much of what happened over the next few days, months and even the first year was a blur.

I felt so bottled up inside because I couldn't seem to cry and I couldn't scream because I was still in shock. All those sad emotions were whirling around in me but I couldn't let them out. I felt that I held myself back because if I started to sob the way I wanted to, I might never stop.

The grief was so hard that I felt as though someone had punched me in the stomach and took all my breath away.

Even though I didn't think you are going to make it through the mass and service, we did manage to get through the viewing and then the next day was the funeral. I kept thinking to myself how will I wake up in time and what if I miss it. I never had trouble sleeping before Chuck's diagnosis but now that he was gone, I would go to bed and start crying until 3 in the morning and then I would fall asleep. Since my schedule was so off, I was afraid I would not wake up in time for the funeral the next day. How strange that I would worry about waking up in time. I was so out of it.

Now, it was the day of the funeral and we all went through the motions of going to Mass and the funeral. It was surreal. I never knew this kind of sadness existed until now. Being in shock is something I had never experienced before and so the feelings I had were new and scary to me.

From the outside, we were all going through the motions of greeting people and getting through the day but inside we were still in disbelief. How long will this disbelief last?

Every night I cried myself to sleep or should I say I cried until the early morning hours when I finally fell asleep for just a few hours.

When I awoke every morning for that first year, I continued to feel that this was all a dream and that he was still here with me. After the first few minutes of waking up and realizing he was gone and this wasn't a bad dream, I felt that pain and sadness all over again. I felt this every day, every night and all day long.

It took many, many months before I woke up and realized that he was gone. It took almost a year before I could accept the reality of his death.

What I found so difficult was to say the word die or death. I could say he passed away but for a very long time those words die or death would not come out of my mouth. I don't know why but that word maybe was too much of a reality or too harsh for me to accept. It was just so final.

It was even hard mentioning his name because I didn't want to fall apart and never stop crying, so just saying his name hurt.

Tears were a new way of life for me now. Everything affected me. My sleep was sporadic and after a year and a half of being Chuck's caregiver, I did end up with walking pneumonia. I did not have time for me while I was taking care of him until now. I didn't have a choice but to rest and I wasn't sure how since I couldn't sleep and I didn't want to live.

I didn't know what my future would bring and how I would adjust to this new life. It scared me and made me realize I didn't feel whole anymore. I had lost part of me and I felt empty inside. Who was I and how am I to go on alone? Do I know how to be myself without him? I was so overwhelmed with the idea that I needed to do everything for myself and wouldn't have someone I love to share my day with and to ask for his advice. I would miss his perspective and opinions about life, our children, business and just everyday life decisions which now became all mine. How could I cope with the loss and what this loss brings? I just don't know how to do "being alone". Now what?

SECTION II

CHAPTER 9
GRIEVING

What is Grieving? It is a cause of deep sadness and in my opinion, it is an emotional response to loss. When you grieve, you are feeling emotions like sadness, distress, hurt and deep pain. There is no standard for grieving because it is a very personal experience and no one can tell you how you should feel or grieve. It is such a personal experience because it is your way of processing what you're going through.

What I feel that I learned from my grief is that you can't worry about what others think. During my grief, some people I knew told me that they felt I should be moving forward within a certain time frame. I found that hurtful although I believe their intentions were good. The reality is that when you're upset and grieving, it makes others uncomfortable and since they are not sure how to respond they say things that can be upsetting.

They truly just want to see you heal. It doesn't work that way and it was difficult to hear those words because the grief is forever in your heart and you will never get over it but you will learn to live with it. Such loss is very hard for someone to understand unless they have been through it. I also found that because I focused on my husband and not myself, my health was compromised. I became ill for a while with walking pneumonia a few months after Chuck passed away. I didn't think about taking care of myself and now I didn't have a choice. Remember to take care of yourself, but also allow yourself to feel and experience your loss. By denying those feelings or pushing them aside, it will just make it harder when you finally face your loss and experience the pain. It will hit you at some point but not until you give yourself that time and space to heal. Some days will be good and other days you will feel as though you never want to get out of bed and you just want to die.

Your mind and heart will be playing tricks on you for a while now and it's okay. You will probably go through most of the stages of grief but you will not go through them in any order. Your grief is very personal and the emotions and reactions to grief will happen when you are ready.

There were so many times the first two years that I would be out at the store or walking on the beach and suddenly out of nowhere came this burst of tears and sadness. It didn't matter where I was or what I was doing but there it was tearing me apart again. It took a while for me to accept that this was going to happen and that this was part of my grieving process.

I would sometimes hear a song from our past or one that had a special memory and I would just break down and want to crawl in a hole and die.

The memories of his illness and what we went through would randomly come flooding back and those memories would hit me hard, anytime, anywhere. I didn't know what to expect, even though I read books on it, but when these emotions happen, you just must let them flow. I found that all I could think about when remembering him was when he was sick and I couldn't access the memories of our normal life together for a long, long time. I just had constant memories of his illness and what we went through.

Part of me was strong and focused and knew just what I had to do. The other part of me was lost and alone inside and more than anything, totally numb to all my memories. I had lost the memories of my life with Chuck leaving on those memories of his illness. Suddenly, after his passing, I found my memory gone, not just memories of him but everything. I struggled to think about recipes and stories of my children that happened during their childhood and I couldn't recall anything. My brain was a blank state.

There were times when one of my children would call me and ask me to give them their favorite recipe, which I had made hundreds of times, and my mind would be blank. I couldn't access those memories and yet when I needed to deal with all the issues of his death and business issues, I found myself focused, determined and more than capable of finalizing all the business issues.

Even though I was focused, I became so tired and emotionally stressed, that I felt myself in an emotional downward spiral. Yet my strength and determination to finalize all the business challenges were completed. This went on for over two years and kept me constantly busy.

My sadness was deep and difficult for me and my family. As the days went on and I tried to cope with my loss, I would suddenly find a glimpse of hope that I would be okay. The moment those good feelings happened, I found that I would be out or at the grocery store and out of the blue my cell phone would ring. I didn't want to pick it up but my instinct was to answer the phone, which I did. I couldn't believe how these random calls were suddenly happening and on the other end of the phone was one of Chuck's friends or colleagues whom he placed in a job years ago. Out of nowhere, came these calls asking to speak to Chuck. Stunned and standing at the grocery store, I was faced with sharing my story of how Chuck was ill and then passed away from lung cancer… there I stand crying and shaking while trying to share my story about Chuck. I felt such a deep pain and sorrow in my heart and yet I had the fortitude to tell the caller the whole story and although, saddened by this news we ended the conversation remembering all the good Chuck had done in his career and how he cared about all the people he placed in jobs. He was the kind of man that not only loved being a headhunter (recruiter) but felt he did something good for every single person he placed in a job. In his heart, he wanted the best for that person and he truly believed the career move would provide a better career and life for his candidates. He was very altruistic and cared deeply about the people in his, life both at home and in business.

I found myself in these situations over and over even up until today which is eight years later. Randomly, I will get a call from someone that knew Chuck but didn't know he had passed away. The impact of those calls is not the same as the first few years, but they still bring back memories and that feeling of loss.

A day doesn't go by when I don't think about Chuck and wish he was here with me and my family. As time goes by, I have found that the pain is not as severe and when I say severe let me tell you it was overwhelmingly debilitating. That moment of his death was unreal and the hardest experience of my life.

Life was not back to normal yet and during the times out of the house, either shopping, walking, buying groceries or any of the normal errands we do, I couldn't stop thinking that the world is going on as it always has and why? I couldn't imagine the world the same as before and everyone around me was living their life as though nothing happened. All I could think to myself was how can the world go on. My whole world has ended and everything in my life has come to a halt. Why is everyone going on with their lives and why do I feel so alone? Why did I expect the world to stop because my world stopped?

This was one of those surprising emotions that I was feeling and it just came out of nowhere. When your world stops and everyone else is living, you feel stunned by the reality of life continuing to go on. I found this so hard to accept and deal with, it just didn't feel right. I wanted the whole world to feel the loss. I just didn't feel part of this world anymore but instead I felt separated, alone and distant. It felt as though I was in a different world than everyone else.

I also found myself losing all confidence in my abilities as a mother, person and just about everything. I felt helpless, hopeless and my decisions were hard and I felt so alone, even though I knew I had my family and they were always there for me. This was different because I didn't have Chuck. I still felt so lost, who could I count on to give me advice and love me and protect me? I didn't have my spouse to share the day with and to ask for help with business decisions and even daily decisions I needed to make. This was a very lonely feeling and it tore me apart.

Another experience I had and this may sound silly because I enjoy cooking, but I lost all confidence in myself about everything and I felt that I couldn't even cook a meal. I found when I wanted to remember what my children did when they were young or share stories of my life, I couldn't access those memories. I felt as though I had lost everything, even my mind.

I find that I am missing him more than I can express. He was always there for me and helped me through the tough times in both life and business. He had a special way of loving his children and helping them the same way. Doing this alone is a tough reminder of how much I miss him every day.

One of the hardest and most difficult times for me was not being able to duplicate him and know what his answers would be when my family needed his advice. I felt so many voids in my life and I felt so inadequate during this time. I wanted to be as smart and capable as he was. I guess I just wanted to be both him and me so my children didn't feel the loss completely. I wished I could be both mother and father but how do I fill his shoes and do both roles? My brain knew this wasn't possible but my heart needed to be more complete in both roles and I couldn't do it.

That's when I began to think maybe it would have been better if I died instead of him. He might be needed more than me and all the thoughts that went on in my head were feelings of loss, guilt, inadequacy, incompetence and I just didn't feel good enough about myself.

I started evaluating my life and my future and I became harder on myself and that wasn't working. The only memories I could access now were the last year and a half when he was sick. I had difficulty trying to remember our lives together before that. I had guilt feelings because I didn't think I was always at my best or doing my best for both of us. I had read in the grieving books that it was normal to start feeling guilty about the past and so I did realize this but those feelings were still there. I couldn't let this get me down. Although, I did for a while and I went over and over in my head all the times I felt I could have been a better wife. I felt this way for a long time before I decided to use my ability to work with energy to get me through these tough emotions. I finally came to understand that this is normal, and I am not perfect, but neither was he! We both loved each other and did the best we could at the time. Neither one of us were perfect and so I had to face the fact that it was okay. Can I move on now after all this self-realization was becoming clearer to me?

What happened with me and I think happens with others, is that when someone you love so much dies, you idolize them and all you can see and remember is how wonderful and perfect they were. This is a good thing but not very realistic. It's good because it helps you hold on to the ultimate love story you want to hold on to. It also helps you appreciate and see that person for all the good that they did rather than remembering the tough times. I think those memories were very helpful to me in getting me through my initial grief.

Although, there comes a time when reality does eventually set in and then life begins to become real. This man on the pillar is still the most important person in my life, but he was real and he made mistakes and he had his good and bad traits. Facing that kind of realization was necessary now. Going through all this taught me that life is about the journey and the lessons we need to learn. It's about the mistakes we made and what we learned from those mistakes. How we deal with them and how we overcame them. I think I was finally beginning to see the light again. I was becoming part of the living.

CHAPTER 10
MOVING FORWARD

Depending on what stage of life you are in when you lose the one you love, when your young, old, married with children or without children, you will experience grief in a different way…but you will always feel that deep loss in your heart. There is the commonality if you lose your soul mate, a child or someone you loved deeply, that the pain will be unbearable. Although with time the pain does subside. The realization of death is confusing and moving forward takes time. I feel there will always be a part of me that seems I will never be whole or the same again. Yet after time has passed and I have connected with my wisdom, I feel strong, have found peace, happiness and a purpose for my life.

I went through a period after my loss of not believing in God anymore. It's not that I truly blamed God, because I know that it's not God's fault, but I needed someone to blame. My emotions controlled my thoughts and I found it hard to smile. Not smiling was the norm for me for quite some time, but there came a time when suddenly, after all this sadness, I found myself smiling. It was the strangest feeling and I thought to myself, I am back to me again. Not sure how I felt about that, but it was happening. I think at first I felt guilty smiling as though I wasn't honoring my loss and how dare I smile. I know that Chuck would have wanted me to be happy, but that was a difficult concept for me to understand then.

That moment was the beginning of my healing because that smile helped me be aware that life was going on around me and I could choose to participate or I could choose to be depressed. I wanted to be miserable and sad forever, which I was for a year, at least within myself. There were many times when I wanted and needed to be unhappy and sad because the pain was so deep and I couldn't imagine ever being happy with all this pain. It was a slow start feeling happy again, because I didn't suddenly smile and then everything was back to normal. Oh, no, it was one day at a time that I was slowly coming back to who I really was. This was important for me to make a conscious effort during the day to laugh, smile and find happiness within.

I knew in my heart that I had a choice and it was time for me to choose to be okay with life. It was time for me to turn this loss around and make it something more positive.

I have learned that I can choose to dwell in the past, or I can choose to move forward. There were times when I thought that I was moving forward because I thought this is what I should be doing. Even though I began by trying to be happy, because of knowing how difficult it was for others, sooner than later, the happiness was taking over the sadness. No one wants to be around someone crying, sad or unhappy.

So many times, I would be okay when I was with family or friends but as soon as I got in the car or walked through the door of my empty house, I would fall apart and sometimes I would cry all night. I wonder how many tears can a person shed? For me, more than I had shed in a lifetime. I realized that I needed to allow myself to have both good days and bad days or good moments and bad moments. So many memories kept flooding in my mind that would bring me down as I was trying to move forward. I realized it was going to still be a process and that my healing was going to take more time.

As time was passing by, I was learning that time does help in the healing process. I was learning to live with my loss but still to this day there is always that place in my heart that is sad and lonely and part of me thinks that I should have that feeling. But I am not sure that I really should hold on to those feelings. I think there will be someday when I'll be willing to let them go. It will not stop me from living and being happy. I do have many blessings and I sometimes feel guilty that I'm still lonely and sad, so motivating myself is important and keeping my attitude positive helps me to keep moving forward.

I believe I have a purpose here on earth and it is learning to love myself so I can learn and help others help themselves. For me to keep moving forward, I focused on my purpose and held onto the good memories Chuck and I had together. I am finally beginning to remember the good times and recalling the funny stories, of which there are many. I had felt lost in this world of who am I without Chuck, but with time, determination and lots of energy work, the old me that was buried for a while is surfacing again and this feels so good.

Once I started opening my heart and my soul to feeling Chuck's presence, my feelings changed and most of the loneliness disappeared. I knew he was here with me, at my side, all the time. I began dreaming of him more often and these dreams did affect my day. Good dreams made me feel happy but sad dreams took me a while to overcome. I found that I could overcome them when I connected with my soul and my higher self. Doing this increased my vibratory level which heightened my awareness and clarity. This was part of the energy work that I had learned before.

When Chuck first passed away, I felt him with me, but then it faded as my grief intensified. I was scared, sad and sometimes angry during this grieving time which I believe made it harder to feel his presence. Although, I have almost always felt his presence, when the grief was so deep, I couldn't feel him. When I opened my heart, and released some of these negative emotions, I could feel him with me again. This was an ah ha moment for me. I found that when I was high and clear it was easy to connect with Chuck, but when I was low and negative, I could not connect with him. Once I knew I could control it, it made me feel better.

My desire to feel him close to me and know that he was right there suddenly became stronger and more powerful than my sadness and loneliness. Once that happened, I felt his presence with me all the time. I didn't always pay attention to that, but I can tune in to him whenever I want to feel him here with me.

I have even heard his voice, not only in my head but also out loud a few times. I find that so comforting. Another way Chuck communicates with me is by turning lights on. The first few years he would turn on a light in my son's house for every birthday, holiday or important event in our lives. One night when I was home alone and feeling quite sad, I was upset with Chuck because he would always turn on the light at my son's house but never at my house. I asked him why don't you turn the lights on in my house? At the time, I was watching TV and just after I asked him that question, my TV started to go fuzzy and it turned off and then it turned on again. I remember saying, is that you? How do I know that's you and then it would happen again? The TV turned fuzzy and then off and then back on again. I knew it was him and it gave me so much comfort to know that he was always here with me even if I couldn't see him.

═══

I have always analyzed my life and myself and I want to know what I need to learn from this loss. I believe there is more to life that just living your normal routine. I think we are here to learn many lessons and to grow spiritually.

I feel that our individual lessons are very personal and unique to who we are. Through these tough times we have choices to make to learn and grow from these experiences, or stay where we are emotionally. There are no set answers and I feel that everyone is here for different reasons and lessons. The beauty of life is that we are all different and we cope with our situations the best way we know how to. It is important to honor ourselves so we can be the person we are meant to be.

No matter what others are doing or how they handle their loss, there is no right or wrong. So don't let anyone tell you when to get over your loss. We all need to work through our grief the best way we can and we will move on when we are ready!

One of the most helpful times for me was when I could share my feelings with a family member or friend and they would just listen. It comforted me to talk about my experience over and over to someone who just cared and listened. It was a good release for me. I felt the more I talked about him and what I went through, the more I felt him by my side.

It is easy to struggle and hold our grief inside. There were times when I just wanted to be mad and angry and feel sorry for myself. That's okay too if we learn that it's okay to take a day or two now and then and feel bad. However, we should try to put those emotions aside because our loved ones would not like to see us sad and unhappy. We will miss them, love them and feel alone on and off throughout our life. Although at the same time, we can take control of our thoughts, our actions, our lives and do something to make the world a better place.

It is hard to talk about what you think and feel after losing someone you love because it's too painful and if we think about it or talk about it too much, we relive our grief over and over. It does subside a bit although it seems to never go away. We just learn to live with it. Sometimes, I want to be miserable and find reasons to be unhappy and sad and other times I don't want to be sad. I needed to choose how I wanted to feel, either to be miserable or happy. I had to ask myself, "how long do I want to feel this way? When will I be ready to understand the lessons that I need to learn from my grief and experiences and when, will I do something positive with it? Either share it with a friend or hold it inside. Do I give more of myself to someone who needs me instead of being in my own world dealing with my grief every day?" Sometimes I overwhelm myself with things to do and groups to join so I don't have to think about it. That is my way of coping. We all have our own ways of dealing with the grief that we hold in our hearts.

There have been so many times I have asked myself, why do we all have to die and go through losing someone we love? What is the purpose of this grief and why can't it be easier? I think it's time to have a talk with God and find out why we need to suffer in grief rather than making this transition between life and death easier. Or maybe we can and just don't re-alize it because we have not been taught that we are allowed to make it easier.

There are so many moments when I just miss him so much that my body aches and my heart hurts. I have so many moments with my grand-children that are the best times of my life. I often wonder why Chuck couldn't be here to share these moments with us. It is difficult to understand some-times why there are such extremes of joy in our life and life can be so wonderful and yet grief and loss is so heartbreaking.

So, what does that mean and how do we cope? It is important to understand yourself and realize that these feelings of strength and weakness will surface from time to time. There comes a time during this grief when we begin to realize or understand that our loved one would want us to be happy and move on. I keep telling myself that when I start to feel down and it helps lift my spirits.

There is no denying that moving forward is hard and sometimes I keep fighting it. Again, it's a mat-ter of when we are ready to let go of the pain and grief and move forward so we can begin to heal. The healing process is so important for your health and happiness. When you start healing you can also help your family heal.

When I remember the first two years, I would say no to evenings out with neighbors and friends and that was so unusual for me. I would normally always jump at the chance to go out. Now, I said no when being asked out with friends. That changed over time and little by little, I started saying yes and creating a new life for myself. I found that even though I wanted to get out sometimes, there was something tugging at me inside that said, "you're sad, and tired, stay home and I did." Then it dawned on me that I was feeling a little bit of depression. I didn't like feeling this way and so I decided to take charge of my life and be happy again. Now I realized that I was just beginning to get my power back. It empowered me to know that I had the right to choose how I wanted to feel. I could feel good or bad or anything I wanted to feel. I didn't have to be stuck in what I should feel. My empowerment felt good and I could feel Chuck being happy with me and for me.

Those moments of sadness and crying were so random for me. I could be walking on the beach and see a couple holding hands and I would immediately feel that pit in my stomach, making me sad and feeling sick inside. I would cry and cry and just have the hardest time understanding why. Why do I have to be alone? There is no question that times like these came frequently and were tough to get through.

For me, evenings and weekends were and still are the hardest. We always kept busy on weekends, even after all the sports and activities for the kids were over. We were both into going out to breakfast, museums, events, dinner and parties, etc. We enjoyed being out together and with others. Staying home was harder for us.

Understanding how active we were together, being alone and not having my partner was unbearable on weekends. At night after being out somewhere when I came back to my empty house, especially during the first two years without anyone to greet me, I felt torn inside and it was such a sad and lonely feeling. Maybe I had a lesson to learn on how to be alone with myself and feel happy and whole no matter what.

I have a fantastic family and there are so many activities that we do together which keeps me busy. I don't know how I would have handled my loneliness without them. My children and my grandchildren light up my life.

After a day or evening out, I would love to have come home and share my day's activities with my husband. Without him here, it hurts and it has taken me a while to process how to be alone.

Even though sometimes I didn't want to live without him, I found that I had a stronger desire to survive and move on. This alone thing is something I had never experienced before. This aloneness is a strange and unique feeling to me. It took me a while to figure out.

I had to begin searching my soul and find me somewhere inside myself. There was a time in my life before we met that I was strong, alone and capable of anything, but the longer we were married we grew closer and became like one. We both knew what the other person was going to say. We were so much better together than alone. It was time for me to find myself again. It took time and I had many moments of despair. I did eventually find me because I was there all along but I hadn't accessed that part of me for a very long time. That's not to say I wasn't independent and had a mind of my own, because truely I did. Learning to be all you can be without the love and support of your loved one was challenging but I finally got it.

With time, I have learned to cope and to be happy again and to make the choice to move forward in my life. I do believe in the power of the mind and that your thoughts do create your life so now it was time for me to create this new life.

What do I mean by that? I mean that I was ready to focus on the good that I have and the wonderful blessings in my life. I had to come to that realization when I was ready and able to accept that Chuck was gone and I was alone. That doesn't mean I don't go up and down with my emotions and my grief, but what it does mean for me, is that I work hard at meditating, choosing to be happy, choosing to see my blessings and deciding to live a good and happy life until we meet again someday.

I also found that I was good at doing things that I didn't know I could do, like handling and running my own business, doing research, giving speeches at big events with crowds of people, becoming better at using the internet, etc. I found that I had more confidence in my abilities then I realized. I have become an independent person again and I like it. I found traveling my life path can be easy or hard depending on how you perceive and handle everything. I love having the power to choose my thoughts and feelings and never have to be stuck anymore.

CHAPTER 11
MY FINAL THOUGHTS

My love story isn't just about the pain and grief I felt every day, but how I managed to emotionally work through each day and how I had to keep my attitude strong and positive.

Cancer is a terrible disease and death from cancer is physically, mentally and emotionally debilitating for all involved. The amount of mental anguish during the treatment stage is overwhelming.

Being a caregiver is difficult and exhausting, but it gave me a new and deep understanding of my love for Chuck. When two people can come together to fight for a life, the immense strength and fortitude you find within yourself is incredible. We drew on each other's love and strength to keep fighting every day for his survival.

In so many ways this time for me was an awakening of every part of my being. From my mind's ability to deny the inevitable to the spiritual strength God gave me to be physically, mentally and emotionally able to get up every day and be positive, organized and focused.

For all of us caregivers, we ask ourselves, "where do we find the strength and persistence to forge ahead every day? How do we keep a positive outlook so we could support our loved ones and stay on the right track so we never give up?" I know that I found my strength in God but more so in the love and support from my children.

The research was immense but the answers were few. I had read so many books on both the medical side and the alternative choices for treating cancer. Is there just one answer for all treatments? No, there were many different choices but none that could cure him just extend his life. I didn't find the answers I wanted to hear because he was diagnosed with fourth stage lung cancer. Since there isn't a cure for fourth stage lung cancer and so many questions go unanswered, we realized that we had to look within ourselves to find the answers on all the choices we had to make. These were major decisions and very scary to think about.

The question we kept trying to find an answer for was, can we prolong his life? Well, I believe we could and I think our story is one that demonstrates how we did just that for an extra sixteen months. We did this through our love for each other, our children's love, our beliefs, the energy work, meditating and the determination to never give up. The medications helped with the pain, although we had to go through different ones before we found what worked for him. The love from family and the will to live was the key to the extra time we had together. But why with his will to live, did the end still come so early? Unless he lived until he was very old, for us it would always be too early. I am thankful that we had more time than diagnosed, since he was given two to three months and he lived for eighteen months. This was longer than the doctors gave him but not long enough since we truly believed he would be cured. No matter how many more months he had, I just wanted ONE MORE DAY.

FEELING THE LOSS

On that very sad day that was my husband's last, I grieved with such intensity that it broke my heart and the feeling of loss I had was beyond my imagination. I could not believe that such pain I was feeling in my heart was possible. It was and how sad that we must experience this pain?

As time goes by, I am learning to live with the loss and trying to continue moving forward with the knowledge that I can do it and I have a purpose in my life. I don't want to feel the loss or sadness and this emptiness that lingers in my heart and soul each day any more. I find that I do great for weeks and sometimes for a month or so at a time and then suddenly one day I wake up and I feel sad all over again and life feels tough and lonely.

I repeat this same scenario over and over and I guess this will continue throughout my lifetime. So, what does that mean and how do we cope? I am finding that I must learn to stay happy and be strong and yet still allow myself to have those times of sadness and to recognize them, deal with them as I choose and then move on. For me, getting back into the social world with friends, being involved with family and being involved with charity work keeps me centered, happy and able to cope.

I have been moving forward these last eight years. My life is back to the new normal and I am happy. Every morning when I wake up, I look at his picture and I think of him, remembering the good, happy and funny times we had. The shift has changed for me and realistically the first two years were the worst, but gradually each year has become easier. I will miss him every day of my life and I will think of him all the time but I know now I can make it on my own and I am capable of being me again.

One of the ways life changed drastically for me was when I realized that I was alone, but also that all the decisions I make will now be mine. I have complete freedom in my life to experience whatever I want to. I don't have to take care of anyone and I don't have to be home at a certain time to cook dinner. I could go out, stay home, travel, move and do almost anything I wanted. So why did this feel so miserable? Why was this complete freedom the scariest and most uncomfortable feeling ever? I think many times in my life, I thought how wonderful it would be if I had these freedoms but when it became a reality, I didn't want it. I wanted someone to love and to take care of and share my life with. This new freedom wasn't for me. This was too difficult an adjustment the first two years.

Of course, I still wish he was here with me and still to this day I even dream about him coming back.

Although I have moved on in many ways, I still suffer feeling alone sometimes. For a long time, I didn't feel complete without him but I have found that part of me that is now complete and whole. I am complete just being me and that feels good. When I have moments of feeling lost or not whole, I become aware of those feelings and choose not to let those feelings take over anymore. I know someday when I leave this world that we will be together again.

These last eight years have been hard but also this has been a time for me to learn about myself and face many of the lessons that I needed to learn. I would sometimes think he would walk through that door and be home again as though he had never left. I wish I had all the answers to life and death and the separation death brings. The loneliness that is deep within me has been easier to deal with since I have connected to Chuck on a soul level every day and truly feel him with me all the time. That doesn't change the fact that he is not on earth with me and that leaves a void but the fulfillment of feeling him around me has given me more peace than I could have imagined.

Now that I have moved on and can feel happy, I would like to end this book with a letter to my love.

My Dearest Chuck:

Every day I miss you and I hold on to our love that is deep in my heart. I think of all the wonderful memories we created in our life and the crazy times we had together.

You will always be my true and only love and nothing can take that away. You're my soul mate, my love, my partner, my children's father. You're everything to me and being without you has left a hole in my heart. A hole that can never be filled.

I know what gets me through each day is the soul connection to you and I know you are with me all the time. I feel your happiness when I am happy and that makes me stronger.

I am moving on and some days I can't believe that I can continue every day with a smile and a will to live. There is always that part of me that is missing you my love, my best friend...and that part still hurts but not as often as it did because I know you want me to be happy and so I am.

I wish I had *Just One More Day.* There would be so much more to enjoy and experience with you here. The hardest part when I look back, is that I could not accept your cancer as fatal and never did until the last three days. By then, I felt it was too late to express all my feelings but looking back I now understand that you always knew how I felt. I love you and always will. I know that you are my angel watching over me and our family. I love you forever.

Love Always,

Debbie

Resource:

Over the years, I have learned how energy aware-ness can change our lives. There are numerous techniques that have truly helped me get through some of the most difficult times.

When the emotional pain became unbearable, I used a combination of various exercises and when I thought I just couldn't do this anymore, using these techniques pulled me through.

If you would like to learn more about the energy techniques I used to get through my life, especial-ly during my caregiving days and my grief, please read: "*The Next Step Up, The Art of Instant Stress Release,* by Barbara Mahaffey, M.A. She is my dear friend and partner in our business, Energy Therapeutic Solutions. Visit our website at etsforyou.com. This book is also available on Amazon.com.

www.ingramcontent.com/pod-product-compliance
Lightning Source LLC
Chambersburg PA
CBHW020544030426
42337CB00013B/974